Nicolas de Freytas

The Expedition of Don Diego Dionisio de Peñalosa

Governor of New Mexico, from Santa Fé to the River Mischipi and Quivira

in 1662

Nicolas de Freytas

The Expedition of Don Diego Dionisio de Peñalosa
Governor of New Mexico, from Santa Fé to the River Mischipi and Quivira in 1662

ISBN/EAN: 9783337042332

Printed in Europe, USA, Canada, Australia, Japan

Cover: Foto ©Andreas Hilbeck / pixelio.de

More available books at **www.hansebooks.com**

THE EXPEDITION

OF

DON DIEGO DIONISIO DE PEÑALOSA,

GOVERNOR OF NEW MEXICO,

FROM SANTA FE TO THE RIVER MISCHIPI AND QUIVIRA IN 1662,

AS DESCRIBED BY

FATHER NICHOLAS DE FREYTAS, O.S.F.

With an account of Peñalosa's projects to aid the French to conquer the Mining Country in Northern Mexico; and his connection with Cavelier de la Salle.

BY

JOHN GILMARY SHEA.

New York:
JOHN G. SHEA.
1882.

Copyright,
JOHN G. SHEA,
1882.

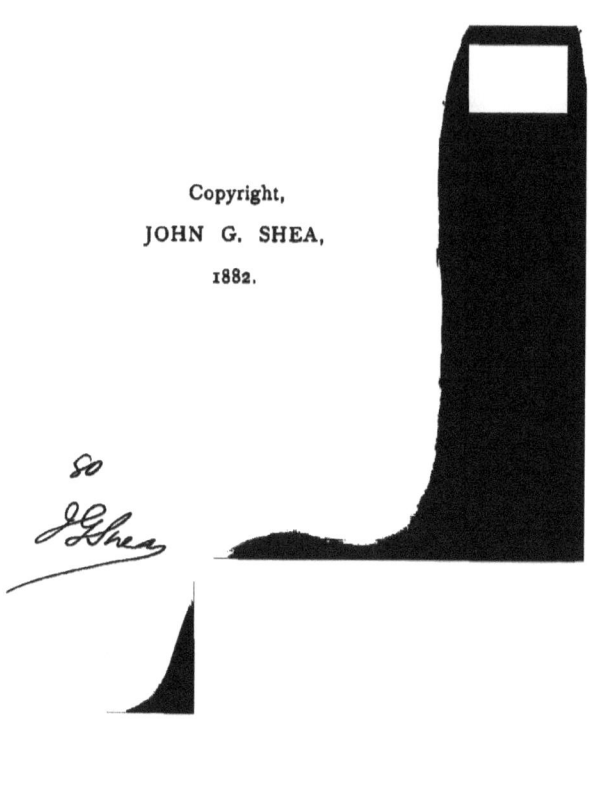

PREFACE.

THE following is a contribution to the early Spanish explorations towards the Mississippi from the west in the sixteenth and seventeenth centuries. It includes the narrative of an expedition which reached the Missouri apparently, in 1662, under Peñalosa, Governor of New Mexico, who, falling subsequently under the ban of the Inquisition, went over to the French and formed a project for wresting northern Mexico from the Spaniards.

In this lies the real secret of La Salle's last expedition, and we are thus enabled to begin the unravelling of one of the most egregious falsifications of history on record.

The French government apparently suppressed all revelations as to the real character of La Salle's expedition, so that the theory of his being carried by the malice of his enemies beyond the Mississippi has been generally adopted by writers.

It is now clear that he went to Texas designedly to pave the way for Peñalosa's projected campaign.

This narrative will help to a better understanding of the early Spanish intercourse with Quivira, and, I think, shows that province to have been north of the Missouri River.

INTRODUCTION.

THE curious, vague, and bombastic account by Father Freytas was found in November, 1856, in the Deposito Hidrográfico of the Spanish government at Madrid, by the late Buckingham Smith.

It had been in the hands of the historian, Martin Fernandez de Navarrete, who made the following memorandum on it:

"A copy of this expedition in modern hand, which has served as an original, is in the possession of Don Bernardo de Yriarte, of the Royal Council of the Indies, who communicated it to me with the greatest complacency, as well as others relating to Quiros, interested in illustrating the history of our voyages. His collection included to the year 1768, but his useful and glorious project was baffled. This copy was compared with the original and corresponds.

"MADRID, July 18, 1791.

"MARTIN FERNZ. DE NAVARRETE.

"This Relation is perhaps the manuscript memoir in French which was in Thevenot's library,. and is cited by Señor Barcia, p. 609 of his 'Epitome of the Bibliotheca Oriental of Pinelo.'"

At the beginning is this note:

"This Relation was given in the year 1684 by the same Count de Peñalosa to Monsieur de Seignelai, Minister of the Marine."

Beaujeu, the naval officer who commanded one of the vessels in La Salle's last expedition, writing to Cabaret de Villermont in June, 1684,* and speaking of La Salle, says:

"He then showed me the article of a Relation of certain Spanish missionaries, which he told me he had extracted from a book in the library of Mr. de Seignelay, which gives a description of his river that he declares to be very faithful, and in fact it agrees very fairly with all that I have heard him say about it, whether he saw the things himself or took them from his Relation, which gives the names of the mines by which it passes, which are fifteen or sixteen, one of which he told me he knew of his own knowledge. The description of the mouth is also conformable to his and to his map."

It would seem probable, then, that La Salle saw this very document, among others, as he was in personal relations with Peñalosa, both he and Captain Beaujeu having dined with that gentleman at the house of a Mr. Morel.†

Who was the Count de Peñalosa?

A document published by Mr. Margry,‡ and apparently drawn up by the count himself, gives this account:

"The Count of Peñalossa was born at Lima, the capital city of Peru, in the year 1624. There are few houses in America as illustrious as his, since he is allied to several grandees of Spain, such as the Dukes of Sessa and Escalona, the Counts of Pieño en Rostro, and the Marquises of Maya. On his father's side he is descended from the houses of Peñalossa and Briseño, Ocampo, Verdugo, and Cordova; and on his mother's side from those of Arias de Anaya, Valdivia, Cabrera, and Bobadilla. Pedro Arias de Avila, first governor of Terra Firma, was his great-great-grandfather; Diego de Ocampo, admiral of the South Sea, and Pedro de Valdivia, who at his own cost conquered the kingdom of Chili, were his great-grandfathers. The Commander Diego

---

* Margry, ii. p. 428.   † Margry.   ‡ Vol. iii. p. 39.

de Peñalossa, his grandfather, son of Alonzo Fernandez de Peñalossa, Knight of the Order of Alcantara, was born in Spain. He went over to America with his kinsman, the Marquis de Cañete, Viceroy of Peru; he held several important offices there, such as those of general or grandmaster of the artillery of that kingdom, alcalde or governor of the forts of the port of Callao, superintendent of the king's fortifications and buildings, general on sea and land, and several others.

"Don Alonso de Peñalossa, Knight of the Order of Calatrava, his father, was maestre de campo in an infantry regiment, commandant of the frontiers in the audience of los Charcos, which is the southern part of Peru, and governor of the provinces of Aricaxa, Arequipa, and many others, and general maestre de campo in the whole kingdom.

"The Count of Peñalossa, at the age of fifteen, was appointed regidor of the city of La Paz; he was then twice ordinary alcalde and thrice justicia mayor in the same city. He raised at his own expense two companies of infantry for the assistance of Chili, and one of eighty men which he led to war against the Chuncho Indians, who 'had revolted, and who were forced to submit. He was soon after made captain of cavalry, governor of the province of Omasuyos, ordinary alcalde of the city of Cuzco, and at last he purchased the office of provincial alcalde of the city of Paz and of the five provinces dependent thereon. This office, which still belongs to him, cost him fifty thousand crowns.

"During the time that he exercised it he quarrelled with the brother of the Count of Salvatierra, Viceroy of Peru. This altercation and the desire of seeing Spain induced him to leave Peru. He embarked at the port of Callao in the year 1652. The vessel on which he embarked foundered in sight of the port of Payta. He there lost more than forty thousand crowns, and saved only ten or twelve thousand crowns in pearls and precious stones.

"He soon after proceeded to Panama, where he resolved to go and see his uncle, Don Alonzo Briseño y Cordova, Bishop of Nicaragua. On his way he was again shipwrecked and with difficulty reached that prelate, who then supplied him with means to go with an equipage becoming his rank to Mexico, capital of New Spain, where, at the court of the viceroy, he awaited news and money from Peru.

"The Duke of Albuquerque was then viceroy of New Spain, and he received the Count of Peñalossa so favorably that he induced him to resolve to remain in Mexico. Soon after the duke gave him two companies of infantry; in the year 1655 he gave him command of all the infantry which he sent to the assistance of the fleet commanded by the Marquis of Montalegre, who had retired to Vera Cruz to avoid the fleet of sixty-eight men-of-war which Cromwell sent to America, and which seized the island of Jamaica.

"During the time that the Count of Peñalossa was at Vera Cruz the same viceroy gave him orders to proceed to Havana with the same infantry, in order to have an eye to the preservation of that important post, in which he remained eleven months.

"On his return the Duke of Albuquerque made him alcalde mayor or governor of the province of Xiquilpa; to this he added the government of the province of Chilcota and the office of his lieutenant-general in the same provinces, situated in the country of Mechoacan, and he gave him several other important offices during the rest of his viceroyalty.

"The Marquis Count de Baños having succeeded the Duke of Albuquerque,* great complaints were made to him against Don Bernard Lopez de Mendizaval, Governor of New Mexico, whose greatest crime was his falling out with the inquisitors and their partisans. Nevertheless he was recalled, and the Count of Peñalossa was selected to command in his stead and to appease the troubles ordinary in that country.

"His commission as governor and captain-general of New Mexico was issued to him at the end of the year 1660, and he proceeded to go thither in 1661. He at last halted for two months at Zacatecas to await his equipage, and one month at Parral, in New Biscay, in order to provide himself with necessaries. He appeased the troubles in New Mexico, made war on the hostile Indians called Apaches, whom he defeated and compelled to sue for peace. He founded two new cities, erected several public buildings, and discovered new countries. But he had the misfortune, as most of his predecessors had, to become involved

---

* Francis Fernandez de la Cueva, Duke of Alburquerque, was viceroy from August, 1653, to September, 1660; and John de Leiva y de la Cerda, Marquis of Leiva and of Ladrada, Count de Baños, held the office from September 16, 1660, to June, 1664.

INTRODUCTION.

with the inquisitors. The commissary-general of the Inquisition assumed a boundless authority and wished to dispose sovereignly of everything; so that, to check his tyrannical and extravagant enterprises, he was compelled to arrest him as a prisoner for a week in a chamber of the palace, after which he set him at liberty, in the hope that he would be more moderate in the future.

"In the year 1664 the Count of Peñalossa returned to Mexico by the ordinary route of Parral, where he spent three months and a half, in order to propose to the viceroy the conquest of the countries which he had discovered. But the Inquisition, which never pardons the least thing done against its supreme authority, had him arrested in Mexico and detained him there as a prisoner for thirty-two months.* It made inquiry into all his actions and all his words, and at last sold all his property for eighty-six thousand crowns, although it amounted to more than three hundred thousand, of which he has the inventories in his power, deprived him of his governorship, declared him incapable of holding any other in New Spain, and condemned him to a fine of fifty-one thousand crowns, and refused to restore him the remaining thirty-five thousand.

"The Count of Peñalossa resolved to proceed to Spain in order to demand justice for such a persecution. He went to Vera Cruz in 1668, and then to Havana to await money from Peru; but his misfortune or the terror and artifices of the Inquisition were so great that up to the present time he has been unable to receive any information from there.

"After waiting for a long time he embarked in the year 1669 in a Canary Island vessel, which took him to the island of Teneriffe, where he was well received by the governor, his kinsman, and by all persons of quality, one of whom, who has recently written to him, has two sons studying at Clermont College, Paris.

"The difficulty of obtaining tidings from his relatives, the Spaniards scarcely sending one or two vessels every year to the Canaries, com-

* "On the 3d of February, 1668, the tribunal of the Inquisition celebrated an Auto de fe in Santo Domingo, in which Don Diego de Peñalosa, Governor of New Mexico, was condemned to penance 'for his unrestrained language (suelto de lengua) against the priests and lords inquisitors'" (Alaman, "Disertaciones," iii., Apendice, p. 36).

pelled him to embark on the English fleet and go to London. There he had the honor of saluting the king and the Duke of York, who did him many favors; he also saw the Marquis de Fresno and the Count de Molina, Spanish ambassadors, who, instead of assisting him, took umbrage at his stay in London and persecuted him anew.

"He accordingly resolved to proceed to France, hoping that the conclusion of peace, which was then deemed very near, would enable him to find some favorable occasion of passing into Spain. He has several times seen the Spanish ambassadors, and among others the Marquis de Los Balbazes, who have only paid him compliments and manifested much distrust at his stay in France, without considering that he was forced to it.

"So many misfortunes and persecutions have compelled him to adopt the resolution of living under the protection of the greatest king in the world while awaiting some favorable opportunity to restore his affairs."

This sketch does not fix the time of his arrival in France or of his earliest intercourse with the French government. We next hear of him in January, 1682, at the time when La Salle, in midwinter, was painfully making his way from Chicago to the Illinois River. The following proposal, evidently from the Count de Peñalosa, was submitted to the French government:*

"*Memoir for the Marquis de Seignelay touching the establishment of a new colony in Florida at the mouth of the river called Rio Bravo, and the advantages which might redound to the king and his subjects therefrom. January 18, 1682.*

"This part of Florida is not occupied by any European nation. It is situated between the twenty-fifth and thirtieth degrees of latitude. The air is very good there and the climate temperate. It will produce,

* Margry, iii. p. 44.

INTRODUCTION. 13

when cultivated, wine and all kinds of grain, fruits, and domestic animals. It is watered by several navigable rivers abounding in fish, most of which empty into the Rio Bravo, which has a mouth more than two leagues wide and a course of more than forty leagues.

"To explain clearly the utility of this settlement it is necessary to state first something as to the French colony of Saint Domingo. This colony now contains five or six thousand Frenchmen and about seven hundred women, without mentioning negroes of both sexes. It began by only fifty men, who were called buccaneers, and who settled there and maintained themselves in spite of the Spaniards. Subsequently, having multiplied, a part devoted themselves to agriculture, and especially to trade in tobacco. The rest, known under the name of flibustiers, are engaged in expeditions at sea. These last are well inured to war and accustomed to hardship and to the climate. Great use can be made of them in that country, but they would be by no means fit to serve elsewhere. They number about eighteen hundred, all good soldiers and sailors.

"The farming of the tobacco has greatly reduced the trade of this colony and increased the necessity of cruises to enable the flibustiers to subsist; but the king having recently forbidden them to cruise, they are on the point of disbanding for want of means to live, which would be a considerable loss and difficult to repair.

"The desire of preserving such good subjects for his majesty is one of the objects proposed by the new colony. For this nothing is solicited beyond the permission to convey them into the country which has been designated, and the offer is made to bear all the expenses of the settlement.

"It takes only ten or twelve days' sail to run from the island of Santo Domingo to the mouth of the Rio Bravo, which not being occupied or frequented by any Europeans, there is no nation that has any right to oppose or complain of it.

"The advantages of this colony are: 1st. That, being at the mouth of this great river, it can there establish an important trade with the neighboring tribes by furnishing them all the goods it could import from Europe, which our Frenchmen can furnish two hundred per cent.

cheaper than the Spaniards, on account of the three hundred leagues overland transportation their merchandise requires from Vera Cruz, where it all lands, to this country. 2d. This colony could very well raise great quantities of cattle and make other goods, besides those which it drew from the neighboring countries to send to France. 3d. As the interior of the country abounds in mines of gold, silver, copper, lead, and other metals, there is ground for the hope that this colony will discover some and derive great advantage from them, after the manner of the Spaniards, besides paying duties to his majesty.

"But the greatest of all the advantages to be derived from this colony is that when these flibustiers are once settled on *terra firma*, under good leaders who offer to take them over, and who have a perfect knowledge of that country, they will be ready for the first war against Spain, and, whenever it shall please the king to permit it, to make an important conquest for his majesty.

"This conquest is that of New Biscay, in which there are several rich silver-mines at only a short distance from the site of this colony, the chief of which are those of Hendehé, San Juan de Guncame, Sombrerette, Soñora, and those of Parral, recently discovered and more abundant than all the others; besides which there are the gold-mines of San Diego and the lead-mines of Sainte Barbe, or Santa Barbara; and all these mines furnish the Spaniards more gold and silver than all the others of New Spain.

"It will be all the easier for the flibustiers to make themselves masters of this province, since it is known to a certainty, from well-informed persons, that there are not more than four or five hundred men able to bear arms, and these so badly armed and so unused to war that two hundred flibustiers will be more than enough to defeat and rout them.

"These Spaniards cannot be assisted from the city of Mexico, which is nearly two hundred and fifty leagues distant, with several desert tracts to be traversed between the two. The largest levy that the viceroy can make at the present time cannot exceed four or five hundred men; and he could not make this levy in less than three months, because there is not a Spanish soldier in that country who is will-

INTRODUCTION. 15

ing to march without a mule to carry him and another for his baggage.*

"The flibustiers, before the arrival of this reinforcement, which they would not dread, would have more than time enough to establish and fortify themselves in the country, and they might easily prevent the succors from entering, there being narrow passages, easy to guard.

"All the Indians, half-breeds, mulattoes, and even Spaniards born in America, called Creoles, are so bitterly opposed to the native Spaniards, whom they call Cachoupins, on account of the ill-treatment that they receive from them, await only a favorable opportunity to rise, which they would sooner do in favor of the French than of any other nation, because they are Catholics like themselves, and have much more humanity than Spaniards born.

"It would be easy for these Frenchmen to preserve the conquest of this province by means of the proposed colony at the mouth of the Rio Bravo, which flows along New Biscay, and by the constant intercourse between this colony and that on the island of Santo Domingo, which would serve as a way station.

"In fine, this colony, whether considered in time of peace or in time of war, is the most useful and easy of all hitherto made, all conjunctures being favorable to its establishment, if it please Mr. the Marquis to grant it the honor of his protection, without, as has been remarked, any help in money being solicited."

After La Salle returned to France in 1683 with the re-

* Events showed that Peñalosa, although long in Mexico and governor of a province, miscalculated alike the energy and resources of the Spanish commanders in New Spain. Before La Salle reached Texas, Don Andres de Ochoa y Zarate, admiral of the Barloven to fleet, captured in September, 1684, a French cruiser off Yucatan and learned La Salle's plans (Barcia, 249). The Marquis de la Laguna then sent Barroto, an experienced pilot, to Havana, with orders to the governor to fit out a frigate at once to run along the gulf coast till he found where La Salle landed (ib. 252). Barroto accordingly, in January, 1686, followed the whole coast, but did not discover where La Salle was; then the Count de Monclova sent vessels with light boats to break up any French settlement (ib. 261, 267). This expedition early in 1687 discovered the wrecks of the *Belle* and *Aimable* (ib. p. 268). Don Andres de Pes followed in June with two frigates (ib. p. 284), and made a second voyage along the coast and about the mouth of the Mississippi in 1688 (ib. 287). When tidings came that year that some survivors of La Salle's party were still in Texas, the Count de Galve sent Don Alonso de Leon with an expedition (ib. p. 287, 295; "Discovery of the Mississippi," p. 208). The occupation of Pensacola and of Texas followed.

nown of having descended the Mississippi to its mouth in the Gulf of Mexico, France was on the eve of a rupture with Spain, and Peñalosa's schemes had already influenced the government in countenancing La Salle's descent of the Mississippi. Both Peñalosa and La Salle laid plans before the government. A "Memoir on the Affairs of America," dated January, 1684,* says:

"The Spaniards having declared war against his majesty, he seems to be fully justified in employing the great means which Providence affords him of profiting by so rash a declaration.

"Among these means, the conquests which his majesty can make in the West Indies might be as advantageous to him and more ruinous to the monarchy of Spain than in any other place where his majesty could attack.

"The great facility which is offered for success also seems to invite his majesty, as may be seen in the sequel of this memoir.

"Some time ago an offer was made to his majesty, in a memoir presented to the Marquis de Seigneley, to establish a French colony at the mouth of the river called Rio Bravo, which empties into the Gulf of Mexico, sixty leagues from Panuco, the last Spanish settlement on the Florida coast; and this not only with the view of carrying on an extended trade, but also to be in a position, on the first declaration of war, to employ this settlement to effect the conquest of one of the most important Spanish provinces, called New Biscay, where there are many mines of silver, gold, and other different metals. These mines are those of Parral, Guincame, Sombrarete, Endehe, San Juan, Santa Barbara, and others, all richer than those of the other provinces of the empire of Mexico or New Spain, because they have been recently discovered and are not yet exhausted.

"What was then proposed as a remote affair can now be executed in two different ways.

"First proposition : One is that, instead of going to settle at the mouth of the Rio Bravo to approach New Biscay, which this river bounds, the

---

* Margry, iii. p. 48.

INTRODUCTION.

offer is made to go straight to Panuco, which, they guarantee his majesty, can be mastered with great ease, from the certain knowledge that there are not more than thirty or forty Spanish soldiers there, and, after seizing this Spanish settlement, to proceed and with the same ease capture the whole province and mines of New Biscay.

" For this purpose it is proposed to collect a thousand or twelve hundred French fribustiers, who live on the coast of Santo Domingo—men well versed in war, accustomed to the climate and mode of life in these countries, and who have habitually defeated the Spaniards everywhere, plundered their towns, and captured their vessels in the Gulf of Mexico, where these fribustiers often cruise. It is proposed to put at their head a chief named Grammont, accustomed to lead them to battle—a bold fellow, whom they willingly obey, and who was in command of many of them at the capture and sack of Vera Cruz, a chief port of the Spaniards, which was effected some six months ago by a Dutch corsair named Van Horn, who had two men-of-war, and whom the said Sieur de Grammont had joined as his lieutenant.

" It is proposed to associate with him, as principal chief and leader of the enterprise, a man of rank named the Count de Peñalosa, a creole born —that is, an Indian of Spanish race—who is descended from the earliest conquistadors of the country ; who, after having held several important offices both in Peru and Mexico, was governor and captain-general of a great province called New Mexico, for which he shows his commissions and attestations of service ; and who has been ruined in those countries by the religious of the Inquisition, who kept him in prison for thirty-two months and dissipated all his property, without his ever having been able to obtain justice from the Spaniards, which forced him to come to France with a view of offering his services to his majesty and proposing to him the conquest of those countries.

" This man is perfectly familiar with the interior of the country, and especially of the province of New Biscay, of which he offers to effect the conquest.

" He believes that he cannot give better pledges of his fidelity than by putting himself, without a single other countryman of his own, among a thousand or twelve hundred warlike Frenchmen, and at the discretion of the French commander, who is to lead them with him, and to whom he says orders may be given to hang him on the first tree, if he fails in any promise he makes.

"He offers not only to make himself master of Panuco, but also to have all necessary provisions brought in by the inhabitants of the country, both to maintain this conquest, where he proposes to establish a French garrison and to intrench himself well, and to march into New Biscay by a route of about eighty leagues, with which he avers himself to be especially familiar, and that he will find no Spaniards to oppose his march ; that he will find the same ease in seizing the mines and province of New Biscay, which, being in extent longer than France, though narrower, has only five hundred native Spaniards scattered through all that country, but almost all men incapable of defending themselves, enervated by pleasure, and who have never had an occasion for war.

"That, being once in that country with a thousand Frenchmen, or even fewer, he will be its absolute master, and will carry off all its great wealth to convey it to Panuco and ship it to France; and that this conquest will be easy to retain.

"That from the province of New Biscay alone can be easily drawn every year from twenty to twenty-five millions of livres in silver bars, which can be transported to France with much greater ease and less expense than it costs the Spaniards, who, instead of sending all the silver they draw from the mines of this province straight to Panuco, have it carried by mules to Mexico, the capital city, which is more than three hundred leagues distant ; and this is done because the viceroy and all the officers of finance are settled there, and they wish to receive their commission on this silver, which they again despatch on mules at great cost from Mexico to Vera Cruz, where all shipments are made on the Spanish fleet, and this port is more than one hundred leagues distant from the city of Mexico.

"As to the facility of the conquest, he avers that the province of New Biscay has no fortress ; that it will be reduced before the viceroy, who is at the city of Mexico, can be informed of it ; that no sooner will the French appear with him before Panuco than all the Indians, meztizoes, mulattoes, negroes, and even the creoles, will rise against the native Spaniards, whose tyranny they can no longer endure ; that these classes seek only to give themselves up to some other Christian nation who will deliver them from the oppression they suffer ; and that the creoles especially are the most embittered against the born Spaniards, whom they call Cachupins by way of insult, because they maltreat them and deprive them of all offices.

"That in regard to the means of maintaining this conquest he will find the same ease, for when once master of the country it will be necessary to publish an exemption for the people from part of the excessive imposts which they pay the Spaniards, and which, besides the feudal services and mining work they compel them to perform, amount to a fifth part of all they raise, which can be reduced to a tenth in order to establish his majesty's authority and make the French nation liked.

"That the viceroy of Mexico cannot put in the field more than five hundred Spaniards, no matter what effort he makes, on account of the small number that there are of them ; and they are scattered over immense countries, where they are required to keep the natives of the country in obedience, so that one Spanish soldier sometimes commands a whole large country ; and that it is a kind of miracle to see how so small a body of men can control such a vast extent of country and so many ill-disposed tribes, and whom they reduce to the last extremity of harsh slavery.

"That this levy of five hundred Spaniards cannot be made in less than six months, not only to collect them from remote points, but also to collect for them at least a thousand mules, which are rare, and which are employed in carrying their silver bars—there not being a single Spanish soldier settled in this country who will be willing to take the field without a mule to carry him and a mule to carry his baggage.

"That unless the viceroy marches at their head not a quarter will ever reach New Biscay, and that in the consternation into which this conquest would throw all the Spaniards of New Spain the viceroy would never venture to go to any distance from his capital, for fear of causing, by his absence, a general uprising of the whole country, now tired of Spanish domination ; and that even if he came with five hundred Spaniards it would not require more than a hundred French flibustiers to check them at a narrow passage in the mountains through which it is necessary to pass on the march from Mexico to enter New Biscay.

"To ensure the success of this enterprise his majesty is asked only for two men-of-war, equipped with everything necessary for this voyage, both for the security of the expedition and to bring back the silver bars which they propose to bring in great quantities from New Biscay, from Panuco to the coast of Santo Domingo, which will serve as a way station, and thence to France ; one of these vessels of thirty-six and the other of thirty guns, which can be sent into those countries under the pretext of serving to guard the French islands, on the present conjuncture of a war declared by the Spaniards, with an order to the Sieur de Cussy, new royal governor of the coast of Santo Domingo, to collect a thousand or twelve hundred fribustiers, with the vessels necessary to convey them into the gulf and six months' stores, which will be easily found in said island ; and two commissions from his majesty, one for the Count de Peñalossa, of governor of all that he shall seize on the terra firma of America for his majesty's service, and the other of king's lieutenant for the Sieur de Grammont, or such other chief of fribustiers as shall be given him by the said Sieur de Cussy, who, having campaigned with them, knows those who are best fitted to command, and will be able to select the most proper men to carry out this enterprise."

The second proposition, La Salle's, need not here be given in full. It supposed the identity of the Rio Bravo and Mississippi ; La Salle was to build a fort on the Mississippi three hundred leagues below Fort St. Louis of the Illinois, where he was to gather fifteen thousand Indians, then sail from France to meet them at the fort with two hundred Frenchmen, and march into New Biscay with this force and conquer the country. For this he asked a thirty or thirty-six gun vessel.

The next month another memoir was presented, in which this appears :

"The enterprise of the Count de Peñalossa and that of the Sieur de la Salle will serve to support each other. The latter will begin next winter to

INTRODUCTION.

spread alarm in the part of New Biscay which lies towards the river he has discovered; and then the Count de Peñalossa, coming to Panuco with the little army of flibustiers, will find more ease in penetrating, according to his design, across to the Pacific; and these two commanders will then be able to aid each other for their common protection, and divide their conquests, according to his majesty's orders, into two fine rich governments, which will bring every year considerable wealth to France and a new glory to his majesty for having extended his victories and conquests to the New World." *

The government finally combined the two projects and sent La Salle to commence operations in Texas and pave the way for the Count de Peñalosa.

La Salle was despatched with four vessels; he stopped at Santo Domingo, as Peñalosa had proposed to do, and, after conferring with de Cussy, was joined by a few buccaneers; but the whole was carried out so feebly as to ensure disaster. †

By a monstrous system of hypocrisy and falsehood it has long been pretended that La Salle was the victim of enemies; that he was carried past the mouth of the Mississippi by the

---

* Margry, iii. p. 69.

† There is a map by Minet, the engineer who went out with La Salle. It is entitled "Carte de la Louisiane," and is described by Harrisse (Notes, p. 203), and was cited by Parkman, "Discovery of the Great West," p. 330, as showing by a cartouche that Beaujeu betrayed La Salle, and, after leaving him in Texas, went to the real mouth of the Mississippi. It is now recognized by him that the visit to the supposed mouth was prior to the landing in Texas, and that in all probability Galveston Bay was mistaken for the mouth of the river (La Salle, p. 367). The placing of the cartouche shows that the map was prepared before the expedition sailed, and I am inclined to think it was drawn up to submit to the government with the projects. It is an elaborate work, and seems to have been based on data furnished by La Salle and Peñalosa. The course of the Mississippi is extraordinary. It runs southeasterly, then nearly west, then turns and runs southeast to the gulf. The Arkansas has three mouths, the branches connecting; Quivira is placed south of its head-waters. North of the Missouri are Pen loca (perhaps Peñaloça) and Les pancaké (perhaps Leskançaké, the Escanxaques of the Freytas Relation). I am indebted to S. L. M. Barlow, Esq., for the examination of a careful copy of the map made for collection under the direction of Mr. Harrisse.

treachery of Mr. de Beaujeu, the captain of one of the vessels. It is very clear, however, that La Salle went intentionally to Texas as part of the operations against New Biscay; d'Esmanville (Margry, ii. p. 515) shows this.

That he expected to be joined there by a larger force under Peñalosa is evident. "He told me," says Beaujeu, "that we were only the forerunners of the man whom we went to see the morning that we dined at Mr. Morel's, and that he would surely follow us the next year with considerable forces; that the Marquis de Seignelay wished it to be this year, and that this had been intended, but that it had been deferred till next year on his asking the rest of this and an experienced man to reconnoitre the parts well."* "We turned all our hopes to the succor that the king might be able to send us from France," says the Abbé Cavelier, "and we awaited it in patience till the end of the year 1686."

What became of Peñalosa meanwhile and of his plans on Panuco is not known. No trace can be found of any such expedition as he projected against that place. The French government, apparently, finding the Spanish government alert and not only watching the Texas coast with successive cruisers, but actually sending expeditions by land to occupy the country, may have seen the hopelessness of all the grand projects against the rich mining district, and abandoned alike Peñalosa in Paris and La Salle in Texas.

La Salle aided the destruction of his party by his utter unfitness for colonization. It is not easy to conceive how intelligent writers have exalted a man of such utter incapacity into a hero. Neither in Illinois nor in Texas did he

---

* Margry, ii p. 428; Beaujeu's Letter, June 5, 1684.

INTRODUCTION.

attempt to clear ground and plant Indian corn or wheat, to supply food or give means for trade ; in neither did he attempt to purchase a stock of furs or other merchandise to send back and purchase supplies for further trade ; in Texas his last vessel lay idle till it was wrecked. He made no attempt to obtain a cargo to send by her to the West Indies, to obtain relief and show what the country would produce. He did not even march with his whole party to the friendly Cénis, and form a settlement near Tonty's post on the Arkansas. He loitered idly around, waiting apparently for Peñalosa.

The mere memorandum in Margry that the Spanish adventurer died at Paris in 1687, the same year that La Salle perished in Texas, is all that we hear of him after the sailing of the flotilla.

He is still a somewhat shadowy form ; but as governor of New Mexico, an explorer of the country eastward to the Mississippi; as one of the earliest to plan a rising of the Spanish colonists against the mother-country, as well as the first to aid an attempt to dismember Mexico; as one whose projects led to the French attempt to colonize Texas for France, Peñalosa deserves to be known. The facts here collected will, it is hoped, receive additions which will enable us to understand more clearly his connection with the affairs of the Southwest.

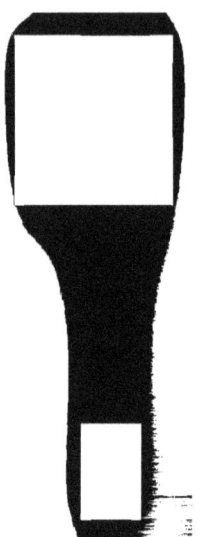

RELACION

DEL DESCUBRIMIENTO DEL

PAIS Y CIUDAD DE QUIVIRA,

ECHO POR

D. DIEGO DIONISIO DE PEÑALOSA,

BRICEÑA Y VERDUGO, OCAMPO Y VALDIVIA, SEÑOR DE LAS VILLAS DE GUARINA Y DE FARARA, Y SUS ONCE PUEBLOS, CAUALLERO FEUDETARIO ENCOMENDADO EN LA CIUDAD DE LA PAZ, ALCALDE PROVINCIAL Y REGIDOR PERPETUO EN ELLA, Y LAS 5 PROVINCIAS DE SU DISTRITO, GOUERNADOR Y CAPITAN GENERAL DEL NUEVO MEXICO; LEGITIMO SUCESOR Y HEREDERO DEL MARQUESADO DE ARAUCO, Y CONDADO DE VALDIVIA (PROVINCIA DE CHILE), VIZCONDADO DE LA YMPERIAL Y MARQUESADO DE ORISTAN, Y PRETENSO MARQUES DE FARARA, Y CONDE DE SANTA FEE DE PEÑALOSA, ADELANTADO DE CHILE Y DE LA GRAN QUIVIRA EN EL OCCIDENTE DE ESTE NUEVO MUNDO DE LA AMERICA.
AÑO DE 1662.

ESCRITA POR EL

PADRE FR. NICOLAS DE FREYTAS,

Del Orden de San Francisco, Predicador y Güardian del Convento do S. Yldephonso en este Reyno, y Capellán de 'SS. Y.*

* " No lo era aun, mas por haver le dicho Yo que lo seria, crehia el estar ya en posesion adelante lo fue."—*Esta nota es del mismo Don Diego de Peñalosa.*

Esta Relacion fue dada el año de 1684 por el mismo Conde de Peñalosa à Monsieur de Seignelai, Ministro de la Marina.

Asi está annotado en Frances en el original de que se ha sacado esta copia.

JORNADA

Del Oriente y Descubrimiento de la Quivira que hizo le Señor Don Diego Dionisio de Peñalosa.

EL AÑO de 1662 á 6 de Marzo salió el señor D. Diego de Peñalosa de la villa de Santa Fee á descubrir las Tierras del Oriente, llevando en su compañia al Padre Predicador Fr. Miguel de Guevara, Güardian del Convento de Santa Fee* y al Padre Fr. Nicolas de Freytas, Güardian del Convento de S. Yldefonso, ambos Religiosos de nuestro Seraphico Padre S. Francisco, el uno por Capellan de S. S. Y. y el otro de la Armada, y una muy lucida compañia de 80 Españoles, entre los qüales hauia *algunos Extrangeros casados en estas partes*, cuyo Capitan era Miguel de Noriega, y su Maestre de Campo Tomé Dominguez de Mendoza, y Sargentos Mayores Don Fernando Duran y Chavez y Juan Lu-

* Del Nuevo Reyno de Mexico.

cero Godoy, y *mil Yndios Ynfantes de Arco y Flecha*, todos muy bien armados, asi las personas como los Cavallos, y con todos los demás Peltrechos de Paz y Guerra, para todos los contingentes que se nos pudieran ofrecer, y con 36 carros y carretas bien probeidos de Viveres y Municiones, y una Carroza, una Litera, y dos Sillas de mano para su Persona, y 6 Piezas de á 3 Libras de bala, 800 Cavallos, y 300 Mulas, y llebabamos la Derrota *al Oriente* hasta havér caminado 200 *legüas*, todas ellas de amenos, apasibles y fertilisimos campos, y tan llanos que en todas ellas, no se vió sierra ni Monte, ó Collao alguno, los qüalés fueron á rematár en un altissima insuperable sierra que está Vecina al Mar, 8 legüas mas alla de la gran ciudad de la Quivira, llamada Taracari, y son tan agradables y fertiles que en todas las Yndias del Peru y Nueva España, ni en la Europa otros Tales se han visto por lo delicioso y ameno, y cubiertos de Bufalos o Bacas de Cibola que causaban notable admiracion, Mientras mas la terra adentro, era mayor el numero, con muchos y muy hermosos Rios, Sienegas, y Fuentes; pobladisimas de frondosas Arboledas y Frutales de diversos generos, que producen gustossisima Ciruela, Vbas gruesas, y buenas con el racimo grande, y de extremado gusto como las de España, y aun excedan.

Muchos Morales para criár seda, Robles, Encinas, Olmos, Fresnos, y Alamos, con otras expecies de Arboles, y yervas provechosas y olorosas, Trebol, Lino, Cañamo, Oregano, que cubria un Hombre á Cauallo, rosa muchisima, infinidad de fresa, aunque menuda sabrosa, muchas Perdices de Castilla, Codornices, Pabos, Gallinetas, Faisanes, Corzos, Ciervos ò Venados en grandisimo numero, y aun casta de ellos tan grandes y crecidos como nuestros cavallos.

Por estos amenos y fertilisimos campos caminamos los Meses de Marzo, Abril, Mayo, y Calendas de Junio, y llegamos á un Rio grande que llaman Mischipi, donde vimos los primeros Yndios de la Nacion *Escanxaques*, que serian en numero de 3 M belicosisimos, bien armados y dispuestos á su modo que iban á dar asalto á la primera Ciudad de los Quiviras, que son sus Enemigos, y se consumen en guerras continuas.

Estos *Escanxaques* despues de Paz dieron noticia de la *Quivira*, y sus gentes, y caminaron con nosotros aquel dia por la Vera de aquel hermoso Rio arriba, que es caudaloso, y hacia en partes muy deleytosas y hermosas Vegas tan fertiles que en algunas se cogen las frutas dos veces al año, y de grandes Arboledas en partes de á 2, 4, 6, y de á 10 legüas, y de Arboles peregrinos y no vistos asta alli.

Desde aquel Puesto torcimos la Derrota acia el *Norte* siguiendo el Rio que trahia su corriente de allá, dexando el Oriente á mano derecha, y aquel dia hizo alto el Real en las Vegas de el, y los Yndios *Escanxaques* se alojaron algo apartados; y fue digno de notar lo que aquella Tarde hicieron, que fue salir hasta 600 de ellos á caza de cibolas, que las tenian bien cerca, y en menos de 3 horas volvieron trayendo cada uno á una, á dos y algunos á 3 legüas de Baca de la increible matanza que hicieron en ellas.

Otro dio marchó el Real, y a 4 legüas andadas descubrimos la gran sierra ya dicha que corria de *Leste* al *Norte* cubierta de humazos, con que se daban avisos de la llegada del Exercito Christiano, y poco despues descubrimos la gran Poblacion ó Ciudad de *Quivira* situada en las anchurosas vegas de otro hermoso Rio que venia de la sierra á entrar y juntarse con el que hasta alli haviamos seguido.

Antes de pasár el gran Rio que nos servia de guia, y á vista de la Ciudad hizo alto el Real en la vega de el, haviendo ordenado el Señor D. Diego antes á los *Escanxaques* que se retirasen y no llegasen á la ciudad sin que su Señoria les mandase otra cosa, lo qüal hicieron, aunque contra su voluntad, porque quisieran que asi ellos como el Señor Adelantado con sus soldados diesen luego asalto á la Ciudad á fuego y sangre y la destruyesen.

Fue tanta la gente que se mostró á la frente de la gran Poblacion, Hombres, Mugeres y Niños, que causó admiracion, y luego vinieron 70 principales Caciques mui bien aderezados á su uso con lindas camuzas y Antes y Gorras, ó Bonetas de Armiños, y dieron la bien venida al Señor Adelantado, con las mayores demostraciones de amor y respecto que pudieron.

Su Ylustrisima los recivió con agasajo, y mandó

que los regalasen, y les dió algunos Presentes con su acustombrada liberalidad, procurando sosegarles los animos turbados por el alboróto que con su vista y la de los *Escanxaques* sus declarados Enemigos havian recibido y ganarles las voluntades para el buen progreso de su Jornada, y dandoles á entender la correspondencia y buena amistad que con ellos tendria, y desde luego enseñandoles no solo con palabras sino con devotisimo afecto y exemplo, hizo érigir el Altar Portatil, donde adoró la Ymagen de Christo, Señor nuestro, y la de la Virgen nuestra Señora, su santisima Madre, y mandó que se cantase Salve y Letanias y después reciviö su Señoria un gran Presente en cantidad de Arminios, Antes, Camuzas, Martas, Nutrias, Castores y Zebellinas, y mucho Pan de Maiz, y en grano, Frijol y calabazas, Gallinetas, Pabos, Perdices, y Conejos y mucho Pescado fresco, que traxeron los Yndios, dando á entender que reciviese aquello en muestras de su voluntad, hasta el dia siguiente que entrase en su Ciudád, lo qüal estaba á la otra vanda del caudaloso Rio, y que eṇ ella le servirian con mucho amór y el regalo posible.

Con esto se voluieron á sus Casas con muy corteses recaudos para los Governadores y Gefes de la Ciudad (que los ambiciosos de pintár testas coronadas en sus Escudos de Armas llaman Reyes). Detubo el Señor Adelantado dos de aquellos principales de aquella Tarde y noche con buenas palabras y mejores obras, fueron examinados y preguntados de su tierra y calidades de ella, y de sus gentes: ellos dieron á su Señoria tan grandiosas noticias y relacion de la tierra adentro que nos causó admiracion; y entre otros muchas cosas dixeron, que aquella ciudád primera que veiamos era tan grande y de tanta gente que en dos dias no le dariamos fin, y que de aquella serrania admirable por su longitud y eminencia que se obstentaba á la vista bajaban muchos Rios caudalosos y pequeños, en cuyas vegas ay Poblaciones de innumerables gentes de su Nacion; que havia gran numero de Lugares grandes, y algunos mayores que el que teniamos presente. Que detrás de ella acia el Oriente corrian otros Rios que entraban en una grandisima Laguna de Agua salada, que corria acia el *Norte*, y no sabian donde terminaba (que sin duda era el Mar del Norte) : Que las Veras destos Rios estaban mas pobladas que su Nacion, y con mayores y mejores Burgos y Casas que las Suyas, y que tenian Rey poderoso que los governaba ; y que á causa de ser mas en numero y poder los tenian y eran sus capitales Enemigos.

Estos son los Ahijaos que poseen las riquisimas minas de Oro, harto mejor savidas de los Yngleses de la Virginia que estan poblados 150 legüas de la Florida, que de los Españoles por su remisa floxedad, y aun se dice que participa Francia de estas noticias por Canada ; y se dice que los vnos y los otros rescatan Metales riquisimos de los Yndios, y que se han visto vender algunos en Roán, de que dió aviso el Archiduque Alberto Conde de Flandes al Rey Phelipe 3° nuestro Señor.

Por lo qüal queriendo deshacer aquella Poblacion de Yngleses, mando S. M. sondar todos los Puertos de la Virginia, encargando aquella conquista a Garibay ; y de por alli cerca acia el *Norte* fue de donde sacó la gran riqueza de oro aquel Corsario Yngles *Ser Tomas* que con increible pujanza y grandeza entró en Londres por el Tamesis con las Xarcias y Velas de seda, y desembarcó y puso en la Plaza de Londres tanto thesoro que la misma Reyna Ysabela con su Corte la fue á vér : y esta cantidad de oro la rescató este Corsario en uno de aquellos Rios que descienden de acia al *Norte* contigüo á esta tierra, que tiene toda su Población *Norte Sur;* y esta codicia ha hecho que los Yngleses ayan querido penetrár la tierra adentro, y por no sabér hacer la guerra á los Yndios han sacado siempre la peor parte, y los tiene tan atemorizados que no osan entrár en Batalla con ellos.

Aqui hemos tenido algunos Yndios naturales de aquellas partes, y que han estado en este Reyno de los Ahijados (que es el Thegüayo) que daban claras señas de ellos, y sus riquezas, y de los Holandeses que alli cerca de la Virginia estaban poblados; y que asimismo hauian estado en las Provincias de los *Otocomanes,* y *Aitacomanes,* donde es tanta la abundancia de oro y plata, que todos los Vasos de su seruicio son de Plata, y algunos de oro; y lo mismo decia (según Personas fidedignas) aquel Yndio Miguel natural de este Reyno de Theguayo que andubo con D. Juan de Oñate, Adelantado del

Nuevo Mexico, al qüal llevó a España el Maesse de Campo Vicente de Saldivar, y en Madrid dio al Rey nuestro Señor estas mismas noticias. S. M. premió el servicio al Maesse de Campo con el Abito de Santiago: y aunque estas ciertas y grandes riquezas se oyen como soñadas entre la poca solicitud Española, entre los Extrangeros están muy vivas, y con evidencia y grandes intereses experimentadas. Por lo qüal no dexan cosa por estas costas *del Mar de el Sur*, *y de el Norte* que no calen y vean, conociendo y estimando mejor que el Español las muchas ricas y grandes Perlas de este nuestro Vecino Golfo de la California, y en las Ensenadas de nuestros Rios, y en especial en los de la Quivira, donde dieron los Yndios tantas (aunque no buenas) al Señor Adelantado, y aqui nos las trahen á rescatar de ordinario, y hemos visto muchas tan gruesas como garvanzos; y de mucho rico ambar que ellos no estiman, y le traen en olorosas Pelotas para sus Entretenimientos. Los dos Casiques prosiguieron diciendo, que mas adelante acia debajo del *Norte* pasados los Pueblos de su nación havia otras gentes ricas y poderosas con grandes Pueblos, que tardarán en pasarlos 3 dias; y todas estas Provincias y las tierras que hemos visto son fertiles, abundantes, frescas y de grandes frutales, especialmente Nogales de 3 diferentes suertes, y muy llenas de *Cíbolas,* y con una gran Laguna circundada de Poblaciones grandes y villages de lucida, rica y belicosa gente.

Duraria la narración de estos Casiques y preguntas del Señor D. Diego y los Padres Capellanos hasta la media noche, hora en que los embiaron á dormir; pero ellos viendose solos y entre gente tan peregrina y extraña, y que su Enemigos los *Escanxaques* estaban tan cerca, se huyeron y pasaron el Rio para su ciudad, la qüal amaneció despoblada y sin gente, porque sus Enemigos los *Escanxaques* sin ser sentidos de los nuestros se deslizaron y dieron asalto en la ciudad, matando, quemando y destruyendo todo lo que podian; á cuyo rebato su Señoria dió orden que el Real pasase el Rio, y se esgüazó con dificultád por ser aun *de noche* y se alojó en la entrada de la ciudad que esta situada en las deleitosas vegas de otro Rio que la entra por medio, y las casas y calles son de la vna y otra vanda, y la fabrica de los edificios por la mayor parte es redonda de á 2, de á 3 y de á 4 altos cubiertos de Paja con admirable curiosidad, y las maderas de Coleo, Curcúra ó Otaté, que todos 3 nombres son de una *caña maziza*, fuerte y nudosa, de que suelen hacer Bastones, que no se cria en tierra caliente; y segun se notó en lo que vimos siembran dos veces al año, porque algunas sementeras estaban para cogerse, y otras se iban sembrando. No se pudó hallar Yndio alguno para lengüa por haberse todos huido temiendo la gran furia de los Enemigos *Escanxaques*, que creyeron que iban favorecidos y aliados con los nuestros, y fue necesario para atajár el incendio de la Ciudad partir la Armada en dos tropas, y que la vna con el Maesçe de Campo se ocupase la mayór parte del dia en retirar los Escanxaques.

La mañana siguiente marchó el Campo por medio de la Poblacion como dos legüas y haviendo contado algunos millares de casas hicieron alto en la orilla de otro Rio que tambien entraba en ella; y se notó que cada qüarto de legüa, poco mas ó menos entraban en la Ciudad caminos Reales de á 16 sendas y algunos de más, muy trilladas, y juntas, que bajaban de la serrania alta que distaria de los edificios como 6 legüas.

Desde aquel parage embió el Señor Adelantado una Esqüadra de 25 soldados con el Sargente Mayor Francisco de Madrid para que fuesen á explorar todo lo Poblado sin poder dar fin á sus calles, y mientras mas adelante reconocian mas poblacion, y mas humazos en la Serrania que hiba por el costado derecho de la ciudad azia el *Norte*.

Pasamos hasta llegar a esta poblacion muchas y muy grandes Rios, que abundan en diversos Peces, como son Bochinetes, Bogas, Matalotes, Bagres, Sardinas, Moxarras, Truchas, Anguilas, Cavallos, Pege-blanco, Cason, Almejas y Camarones, y otros y los mas destos Rios altisimos para sacar Asequias de riego, y las Tierras negras, fuertes, fertiles, y cubiertas de yerva, y en conclusion toda la campiña que habia desde la ciudad de la *Quivira* hasta la sierra, que serian 6 ó 7 legüas, parecia un Paraiso, y viendo el Señor D. Diego que era inutil seguir á quien huia, y que no se savia si el Carruaje hallaria paso, y lo principal por no tener orden de hacer nuevos descubrimientos, desde alli dió la buelta para estas Provincias á 11 de Junio, dia de S. Bernabé, Apostol; y viniendo caminando le salieron al encuentro de mano armada los *Yndios Escanxaques* que ingratos del agasajo que se les havia hecho, haviendose juntado con otros de su nacion, que formaban un cuerpo de mas de 7 M se havian buelto á entrar en la Ciudad ó su frente; y aunque fueron requeridos con la paz no la quisieron admitir, y fue forzoso peleár y en un sangriento combate que con ellos tubo, les mató el Señor Adelantado en menos de 3 horas mas de 3 M, y los demas se pusieron en huida, haviendo experimentado las Ventajas de las valas á las Flechas, aunque ellos las disparan á dilubios, pues parecen tempestades de granizo.

Hallaronse en esta Jornada Hombres de diversas naciones de Europa, Asia, Africa y America, y todos a una voz decian que no hauian visto tierra tan fertil, amena y agradable, como aquella, y están aguardando la buelta de su Señoria con los nuevos ordenes de S. M., y merced de titulo de **Duque** de ella, Marques de Farara, y el de Conde de Santa Feé de Peñalosa, que tan merecido tiene. De alli a 4 meses vino a este Reyno un Casique principal de la *Quivira* con mas de 700 Yndios y Reqüas de Perros cargados de Antes, y Camuzas y otras Pieles, y fué á ver el Señor Adelantado y dió a su Señoria las gracias por el castigo que habia echo en sus Enemigos los *Escanxaques* y de nuevo notició de las grandes y ricas ciudades de la tierra adentro, y cosas notables de ellas, y con el dedo de la mano pintó en el suelo un Mapa, asi de su tierra y Poblaciones vecinas á ellas, como de las de sus Enemigos, y otras con sus Rios, Montes y llanos, ciudades y Pueblos de diferentes edificios, y sus campiñas llenas de *Cibolas* y otras diversas especies de Animales no conocidos en nuestra Europa, con otras cosas de estraña grandeza.

Todo lo qüal asi como el Cacique lo pinto en el suelo lo mandó el señor D. Diego copiar en Papél para remitir á S. M. y rogó el Cacique á su Señoria que volviese á su tierra donde seria mejor recibido que la primera vez, y para guias dejó dos Yndios de su compañia que lo condugesen por menor y mas breve camino. El partió agradecido y contento por el agasajo que su Señoria le hizó dandole un Vestido con una vanda de oro y un sombrero con plumas que le admiró por no ser mas finas las que ellos usan, y un Espadin dorado de que hizo notable estimacion el Barbaro Capitan.

Por lo dicho se ve claramente que todas las noticias que dieron al bendito P. Fr. Francisco de Escobar, y al Adelantado del Nuevo Mexico D. Juan de Oñate qüando conquistó este Reyno, y las que en esta Jornada del *Oriente* y *Quivira* se han dado, hieren todas en una misma parte, que es debajo el *Norte;* y las que los Yndios *Thaos*, y los de la nacion *Apaches*, sus vecinos y mas *Nordestales* nos dan, son todas unas; y que esta tierra Nordestal tan poblada y rica comienza en los espaciosos campos de Quivira 150 legüas de aqui, y se sigue hasta donde empieza lo poblado casi otro tanto; y de alli es increible la grandeza del Pais y Pueblos acia debajo del Norte, todo cercado de Mar por todas partes, y segun la relacion de los Moradores de la del súr dá buelta el Mar por la punta de aquella Sierra de la California, rodeando la tierra acia el Norueste, Norte y Nordeste, y dicen que saben que llega hasta alli y que presumen que pasa adelante, porque no le hallan el ultimo termino; y dan razon de la riquisima Laguna de Copala y sus Mexicanos, que en todo su gran contorno tienen muchas Poblaciones, y desde aquella Laguna acia el Norueste ponen todas las Naciones referidas en la Jornada del Mar del Súr, y los de la Quivira que abitan al Leste dicen que el Mar dista 10 legüas detras de la gran sierra, que esta 8 de la ciudad de Taracari, y que de alli corre acia el Nordeste, y Norte y Norueste, que es el mismo brazo de la California, de suerte que desde Quivira se save con evidente prueba que el Mar ciñe y abraza toda esta Tierra por estos 4 vientos; desde el Leste al Nordeste, y Norte y Norueste.

Y esta eminentisima sierra le va siguiendo siempre, y los Moradores de aquellas Regiones no saben donde terminan; y si desde este Puerto del Nuevo Mexico se mira al Oriente, ó al Norte, ó al Poniente por todas partes hallaremos el Mar á menos de 250 legüas por el circulo uniforme que viene haciendo el de la California por los 4 vientos dichos, y toda la fuerza de riqueza y grandes Poblaciones de esta sierra vecina á la gran Quivira, y mas Oriental son acia el Már, cuyas vertientes á el están pobladas de muchas Ciudades de curiosos Edificios de á 3 altos, y asi va toda la tierra casi corta á costa, riquisima y muy habitada hasta la gran Laguna de Copala de cuyas Minas son las ricas Piedras de oro que el Señor Governador compró á rescate; y aunque toda esta longitud de Poblacion es como se refiere, no debe tener de latitud mas de 50 legüas al modo del Reyno de Portugal, que con ser tan estendido que llega desde la Raya del Reyno de Galicia asta el Algarbe, no tiene de ancho mas de 30 legüas. Y para ser mas breve esta Jornada y descubrimiento, segun dicen los Quiviras, se ha de yr por los Thaos que es camino mas corto ó menos dilatado, y las Poblaciones están mas cercanas; y se entiende y aun tiene por cierto que los 9 Pueblos grandes, que estan de aqui 70 legüas en la derecera de los Tahos acia el Norte, son principio de aquellos extendidos Reynos, y que desde alli se sigue lo poblado, y mientras mas adelante son las Aldeas en mayor numero.

Compruevase también lo referido de la grandiosidad y riqueza de esta tierra Nordestal adentro con las noticias que también hemos leido del viage del Maestre de Campo Vicente de Saldivar, que hizo al Mar del Súr por orden de su Tio el Adelantado D. Juan de Oñate, con piloto y todos los aprestos para fabricar un Barco ó chalupa, mandandole que llegado al Rio de Buena Esperanza (ó del Tison, que todo es uno) no siguiese el Rio abaxo que corre Norte sur acia el Golfo de la California, que es por donde fueron la primera vez, sinó que pasado el Rio con la gran serrania, por cuyas faldas lleva su corriente hasta el Mar del sur, desde aquella sierra bajasen luego al Mar, y buscasen la Ysla de las Gigantas tan nombrada y descubriesen la Laguna de Copala, donde son las riquisimas Minas de Moctegsuma, que con el favor de Dios esperamos ver descubiertas por el señor Adelantado, como se ha escrito.

Una copia de letra moderna de esta Jornada que há servido de original posee Dⁿ Bernardo de Yriarte, del R^l Consejo de la Yndias, que me la há franqueado con la mayor complacencia, igualm^{te} que otros relativos á Quiros interesado en ilustrar la Historia de nuestros viages, cuya colleccion emprehendió por los años de 1768, habiendose malogrado tan util y glorioso proyecto. Se ha confrontado esta copia y queda conforme.

MADRID, 18 de Julio de 1791.

MARTIN FERN^z DE NAVARRETE.

Acaso es esta Relacion la Memoria MS. en Francés que se hallaba en la Libreria de Tevenot, y cita el Sr Barcia en el fol 609 de su epitome á la Bib^{ca} Occidental de Pinelo.

(RUBRICA DE NAVARRETE.)

True copies of the transcripts in the Déposito Hidrográfico of the Spanish government.

The above certificates are on the last page.

Nov. 6, 1856. MADRID.

BUCKINGHAM SMITH.

NOTICIA

de otra Expedicion anterior por el Maestre de Campo Vicente de Saldivár.

El año de 1618 saltó el Maestre de Campo Vicente de Saldivar al descubrimiento de esta Jornada con 47 soldados bien aprestados, y con ellos el Padre Fr. Lazaro Ximenez del orden del nuestro Seraphico Padre S. Francisco, y pasando por estas mismas Naciones pobladas y politicas hasta la ultima de Moq, y caminando por aquellos despoblados otras 15 Jornadas, llegaron al Rio de Buena Esperanza ú del Tison, en el qüal paraxe se hallaron en 36 grados y medio; y caminando por el arriva dos Jornadas acia el Norte con muy buena guia que se ofréció á llevarlos, llegaron á una pequeña Poblacion, y informandose de la tierra adentro, les dixeron tantas grandezas de ella, como les habian dicho los del Poniente en las costas del Mar del Sur y la. California, y como nos dixeron á nosotros la del Oriente en la Quivira, que animo grandemente á todos á seguir su viage; pero como entre las demas cosas les dixeron que adelante hallarian unas gentes terribles y giganteas, tan corpulentas y descomunales que un Hombre de los nuestros á Cavallo era pequeño en su comparacion, y que tiraban grandisimas Flechas, pareciendole á Saldivar no llevar fuerza suficiente para contra tanta multitud de gentes barbaras, y tales que determino volverse temiendo algun mal suceso, como lo espérimentó el Capitan Humaña y otros; y auuque á este parecer resistieron el P. Fr. Lazaro, y los mas de los soldados no bastó, ni aunque se ofrecieron 25 de ellos pidiendole licencia para entrár y calár la tierra, no quiso el Maestre de Campo concedersela, temiendo se perderian todos; antes mandó alzar mano de la Jornada, y volverse; y executando este prudente determinacion, y estando cargando el Bagage, hizó en aquel punto la tierra gran sentimiento con un terrible y espantoso temblór, que parecia jugar con los Montes mas encumbrados segun los messia, derribando por el suelo las Bestias cargadas, y los Hombres sin que quedase cosa en su lugar, mostrando misteriosamente el Cielo con este terremoto la cobardia de animo de los que se volvian desde las Puertas de aquella fertil, rica, y espaciosa tierra, que en el comun sentir todo lo que hasta oy está conquistado y poblado debaxo del nombre de America es sombra en comparacion de lo que contiene esta nueva parte del Mundo nuevo, amenazada de conquistar por los Franceses que confinan con ella, y de los Yngleses y Olandeses que tanto la desean, aunque no lo consiguirán los vnos ni los otros, porque ignoran el Arte de conquistar, reservado al valór y destreza de nuestra nación y la Portuguesa, aunque entonces los Nuestros no osaron llegar lo á ver, siquiera para desengañarse.

Entonces el Padre Fr. Lazaro, dicen, que exclamó diciendo en altas voces con estrañable dolor: Ha Españoles! que la tierra hace sentimiento de nuestra falta de valór, y no lo hacemos nosotros! pero yo creo y lo tengo por sin duda que como nuestro buen Dios y Señor güardó la conquista de la Tierra-firme para el Ylustre Pedrarias de Avila, hijo del Conde de Puñon-rostro, y la del Perú para el bien afortunado Francisco Pizarro y la de Chile para el ynsigne Pedro Gutierrez de Valdivia, y la de la Nauegación del Már del Súr para el famoso D. Diego de Ocampo, y la de Mexico para el inclito Fernán Cortés; guarda esta para el excelente D. Diego Dionisio de Peñalosa, que como Bis-nieto de los tres mayores Cavalleros (Pedro Aries Davila, Pedro de Valdivia, Diego de Ocampo) y mejores soldados de los cinco expresados, y Marido que fué de Nieta del siempre vencedór Marqués del Valle, Duque de Terra-noba (Fernan Cortés) parece que reproduce el valor de tan excelentes Heroes, pues en su tiempo vemos vencidas tantas dificultades y descubierto el camino de propagár el Evangelio, extendér la Monarchia y aumentar el comercio de la Christiandad, haciendo su casa mas ylustre por su Espada con los Titulos de Marqués y Conde, de Vellas Villas que ha fundado desde las primeras piedras, y el que pretende de Duque para hacerse por si tan ylustre como los Excelentisimos de sus gloriosos Progenitores, de cuyos Titulos de Marqués, Conde y Vizconde es legitimo heredero, como del celo en honrár y patrocinár nuestra Seraphica orden, como tan Christiano Cavallero y Hermano nuestro por letras patentes de nuestro Reverendissimo Padre Comisario Genéral, Fr. Diego Zapata.

NOTA.

Este escrito se ha copiado á la letra del que el Padre Gùardián, Predicador y Comisario Fr. Nicolas de Freytas escribió de su mano, el qùal se remitio originál á S. M. con el Memorial impréso del Señor Adelantado el año 1663, cuya resulta se espera para conseguir tan gloriosa empresa dando á la Corona de España Thesoros para dominar al Orbe, á gloria de Dios en cuya mano poderosa están todas las cosas pasadas, presentes, y venideras ; y de su vendita Madre la Virgen Maria, Señora nuestra, concebida sin mancha de pecado original.

Naciones conocidas que trafican con las *Quiviras* y *Ahijaos* del Reyno de Thegüayo cercano á las tierras de los Franceses que llaman de la Canadá en las Riveras del Rio de S. Lorenzo, que nuestros saluages afirman ser muy grande y navegable hasta el Mar, son las siguientes. *Escanxaques* que hacen gran cantidad de Antas blancas y bien curtidas y muchisimas camuzas y otras Pieles, y *yacen en* 40 *Grados* de latitud.

Tienen al Norte la *Tierra del Fuego*, y mas alto la *Laguna dulce*, que dicen es de excesiuo grandór, y en ella desagüa otra Laguna que llaman *Puela*, en que hay una Ysla Minerál de rico cobre, oro bajo, ó Laton subido.

Caminando de los *Escanxaques* para la Nueba Francia, yacen los *Neutrios, Antovorinos, Cavellos Realzados del Mechon del Perun* (yerba que trafican entre ellos y la vsan como tabaco) y los mas feroces los Hiroquees, para los qüales dicen por proberbio; *á* 10 *Hiroquees* 4 *del Mechon, y a estos dos Escanxaques, y a* 10 *Escanxaques un Apache;* todos los qüales son poblados, y algunas de sus Poblaciones cercadas de palizadas á manera de los *Sunis* de nuestra *Cibola*.

Notese que según el Hacho, Reyezuelo, Estanxaque, desde los Hiroquees no dista mucho el

Reyno de la Nueva Francia, que por otro nombre llaman Acanadá, que no seria dificil saquearles las Villas principales.

Notese asimismo que pasada la sierra alta de los *Escanxaques*, á 8 ó 10 Jornadas hay Poblaciones de gente blanca y rubia, que sin duda son Yngleses, de la Virginia ú de la Nueva Ynglaterra. Quiera nuestro Señor por su infinita misericordia, que nuestro Governador y Capitan General allane con su valor y su industria todas las dificultadas, que oponen los que no estan acostumbrado á vencér ymposibles, como lo está su Señoria, para qui en la Divina Providencie, ha guardado en sus senos ocultos hasta este tiempo, *Quia omnia in tempore suo querentur.*

NOTA PUESTA POR EL CONDE DE PEÑALOSA.

Vuesa Paternidad no ha dicho en este Traslado lo de la Etimologia de los nombres de la tierra que havitan los Franceses; con que se prueba la opinion contraria del Governador de la Vizcaya, por que á toda su Tierra de Nueva Francia, la llaman

Canada; diccion corrumpida en su manera de hablar; pues debe decir *Aca-nada*, despreció que hicieron Españoles que la abandonaron por Pobre; y la Vanidad de que blasona el Autor Francés que en el Governador me cita de ser el primero que eligió el sitio en que fundó la capitál de la Acanada, tambien es presumpción sin fundamento, pues por el mismo nombre que el dice, le dan los Yndios Salvages, seconoce haver sido sitio elegido por Españoles, cuya lengüa ignoraba el Capitan Francés como nosotros la suya; es pues Estadaca que sin duda fue persuación (para poblar alli) del Gefe de la Jornada; y haviendo hallado las ruinas el Francés pobló, y le llaman *Quebec*, que no se lo que significa, aunque se puede buscár en el Bocabulario de estas dos Lengüas que embié a V. P. D. y al Padre Guevara que es Cathalán puede ser lo sepa.

RELATION

OF THE DISCOVERY OF THE

COUNTRY AND CITY OF QUIVIRA,

MADE BY

DON DIEGO DIONISIO DE PEÑALOSA,

BRICEÑA Y VERDUGO, OCAMPO Y VALDIVIA, LORD OF THE CITIES OF GUARINA
AND FARARA, AND OF ITS ELEVEN TOWNS, FEUDATORY COMMENDA-
TORY KNIGHT IN THE CITY OF LA PAZ, PROVINCIAL ALCALDE
AND PERPETUAL REGIDOR THEREIN, AND IN THE FIVE
PROVINCES OF ITS DISTRICT, GOVERNOR AND
CAPTAIN-GENERAL OF NEW MEXICO,
LAWFUL SUCCESSOR AND HEIR OF THE MARQUISATE OF ARAUCO, AND THE
COUNTSHIP OF VALDIVIA (PROVINCE OF CHILE), VISCOUNTSHIP OF
LA YMPERIAL, AND MARQUISATE OF ORISTAN, CLAIMANT
OF THE MARQUISATE OF FARARA, AND COUNTSHIP
OF SANTA FEE DE PEÑALOSA, ADELANTADO OF
CHILE AND OF THE GRAN QUIVIRA IN
THE WEST OF THIS NEW WORLD
OF AMERICA, IN THE
YEAR 1662.

WRITTEN BY

FATHER FRIAR NICOLAS DE FREYTAS,

*Of the Order of St. Francis, Preacher, and Guardian of the Convent of San
Ildephonso in this Kingdom, and Chaplain of His Most
Illustrious Lordship.**

* He was not yet so, but as I had said that he should be, he thought himself already in possession. He became so subsequently.—*Note by Peñalosa.* Of this Father, Señor Icazbalceta obligingly sent me the following from Beristain, corrected: "Freitas (Father Nicholas de), Franciscan religious of the Strict Observance, Commissary Visitor of the Third Order in the province of the Holy Gospel in Mexico, published: 'Musica Sagrada en tritono Metaphorico, Sermon que predicó el R. P.... dia de la Santísima Trínidad en la Santa Iglesia Metropolitana de México.' Mexico, Viuda de Bernardo Calderon, 1680. 4°."

EXPEDITION TO THE EASTWARD

And Discovery of Quivira, made by Don Diego Dionisio de Peñalosa.

In the year 1662, on the 6th of March, Señor Don Diego de Peñalosa set out from the city of Santa Fée to discover the lands to the eastward, taking in his company Father Preacher, Friar Michael de Guevara, Guardian of the Convent of Santa Fee,* and Father Friar Nicolas de Freytas, Guardian of the Convent of San Ildefonso,† both religious of our Seraphic Father, Saint Francis, the one as chaplain of his illustrious Lordship, and the other as chaplain of the force, and a very brilliant company of eighty Spaniards, among whom were some foreigners married in these parts, whose cap-

---

* In the new kingdom of Mexico.

† The mission of San Ildefonso among the Teoas Indians was the first established in New Mexico. Benavides, " Memorial," p. 28.

tain was Michael de Noriega, and his Maestre de Campo Thomas Dominguez de Mendoza, and sergeant majors Don Fernando Duran y Chavez and John Lucero Godoy, and a thousand Indians on foot with bows and arrows, all very well armed, both men and horses, and with all the other equipments of peace and war, for all contingencies that might befall us, and with thirty-six carts of various sizes well provided with provisions and munitions, and a large coach, a litter, and two portable chairs for his person, and six three-pounders, eight hundred horses, and three hundred mules; and we took our course eastward till we had marched two hundred leagues, all through pleasing, peaceful, and most fertile fields, and so level that in all of them no mountain, or range, or any hill was seen, which finally ended at a very high and insuperable ridge which is near the sea, eight leagues beyond the great city of Quivira, called Taracari; and so agreeable and fertile are they that in all the Indies of Peru and New Spain, nor in Europe, have any other such been seen, so pleasant and delightful, and covered with buffalo or cows of cibola which caused notable admiration. The further we entered the country the greater was the number, with many and very beautiful rivers, marshes, and springs; studded with luxuriant forest and fruit trees of various kinds, which produce most palatable plums, large and fine grapes in great clusters and of extremely good flavor, like those of Spain, and even better. Many mulberry-trees to raise silk, oaks, evergreen oaks, elms, ash and poplar trees, with other kinds of trees, with useful and fragrant plants, clover, flax, hemp, marjoram high enough to hide a man on horseback, abundance of roses, strawberries without end, small but savory, many Castilian partridges, quails, turkeys, sandpipers, pheasants, deer, stags or elk in very great number, and even one kind of them as large and developed as our horses.

Through these pleasant and most fertile fields we marched during the months of March, April, May, and the kalends of June, and arrived at a large river which they call Mischipi,* where we saw the first

---

* Sagean, pp. 27, 32, put his Acaaniba on the river Milly. La Hontan puts the tribe of Essanapes on his Long River. Zarate Salmeron (cited by

Indians of the Escanxaques nation, who might be to the number of 3,000, most warlike, well armed and equipped in their manner, who were going to attack the first city of the Quiviras, who are their enemies, and are destroying themselves by continual wars.

After entering into peace with us these Escanxaques gave notice of Quivira* and its peoples, and they marched with us that day up by the borders of that beautiful river, which is rapid, and forms in parts very delightful and beautiful prairies, so fertile that in some they gather the fruit twice a year, and great forests in parts at distances of two, four, six, and ten leagues, and strange trees not seen until this place.

Dunbar), in his account of New Mexico, says the Escanxaques were at 46° N. 162° W., and that their country extends obliquely to the shelter formed by certain mountain sides and to a river which flows N.E.–S.E. (? S.W.), and incorporates with another which discharges into the Mississippi. *Magazine of Am. Hist.*, iv. p. 280.

* Coronado in his expedition in 1542 reached Quivira. He puts the great river at 36° N. and Quebira at 40°. He marched 330 leagues from the Rio Grande to it, but his return march was more direct and took only 200. Buck. Smith, "Coleccion," p. 153. There can be little doubt but that the same Quivira was reached by both Coronado and Peñalosa. Minet in his map (Harrisse, p. 203) puts Quivira south of the Arkansas, but seems to place the Escanxaques (Les pancaké) and a place intended for Peñalosa north of the Missouri.

From this point we turned our route northward, following the river which drew its current from thence, leaving the East on our right, and that day the army halted in the prairies by the river, and the Escanxaques Indians lodged somewhat apart; and it is worth noting what they did that evening, which was their going out to the number of six hundred to hunt cibolas, which they found very near, and in less than three hours they returned, each bringing one, two, and some three cows' tongues from the incredible slaughter which they made of them.

The next day the army marched, and after going four leagues we discovered the great range already mentioned which ran from East to North, covered with smokes, by which they gave notice of the arrival of the Christian army, and soon after we discovered the great settlement or city of Quivira, situated on the wide-spread prairies of another beautiful river which came from the range to enter and unite with that which we had hitherto followed.

Before crossing the great river which served us

as a guide, and in sight of the city, the army halted in the prairie thereof, Don Diego having previously ordered the Escanxaques to retire and not enter the city till his Lordship commanded otherwise. This they did, though against their will, because they wished that both they and the Señor Adelantado with his soldiers should at once assault the city with fire and blood, and destroy it.

So numerous were the people who appeared before the great settlement, men, women, and children, that it excited wonder, and then seventy head chiefs came very well attired in their style with neat chamois and buckskin, and caps or bonnets of ermine, and they welcomed the Señor Adelantado with the greatest marks of love and respect that they could.

His Illustrious Lordship received them with pleasure and ordered them to be entertained, and he gave them some presents with his accustomed liberality, endeavoring to quiet their minds, which were disturbed by the alarm which they had felt on seeing him and the Escanxaques, their avowed enemies, as well as to gain their good-will for the furtherance of his expedition, and giving them to understand the friendly intercourse that he would maintain with them, and from the outset impressing this on them not only by words but also by most devoted affection and example. He caused the portable altar to be set up, where he reverenced the image of Christ our Lord, and that of the Virgin, our Lady, his most holy Mother, and ordered the Salve and Litany to be sung, and afterwards his Lordship received a present of a great quantity of ermine, buckskin, chamois, marten, otter, beaver, and sable-skins, and a quantity of Indian corn in grain and bread, beans and pumpkins, sand-pipers, turkeys, partridges, and rabbits, and much fresh fish which the Indians brought, giving him to understand that he should receive that as a mark of their good-will till next day, when he might enter their city, which was on the other bank of the rapid river, and that they would serve him with much love and all possible hospitality.

With this they returned to their houses with very courteous supplies for the governors and chiefs of the city (whom those who are ambitious of painting crowned heads on their coats-of-arms call kings). The Señor Adelantado detained two of those chiefs that evening and night with fair words and better deeds; they were examined and questioned as to their land and the qualities of it and of its tribes. They gave his Lordship such grand accounts and relation of the interior country that it excited our admiration, and among many other things they said that that first city which we saw was so large' and of so great a population that we could not reach the end in two days, and that from that elevated range, wonderful for its length and height, which displayed itself to our sight, many rivers, large and small, descended, on the banks of which are towns of countless tribes of his nation; that there were a great number of great towns and some larger than that we had before us. That back of it eastward ran other rivers which entered a very large lake of salt water, which ran northward, and that they did not know where it terminated (which doubtless was the North sea); that the banks of these rivers were more densely peopled than his nation, and with larger and better towns and houses than his, and that they had a powerful king who governed them, and that on account of their exceeding in numbers and power they regarded them and they were their deadly enemies.

These are the Ahijaos,* who possess the richest gold-mines, much better known by the English of Virginia, who are settled 150 leagues from Florida, than by the Spaniards on account of their remiss lack of energy, and it is even said that France also shares in this information through Canada; and it is said both nations obtain very rich ores from the Indians, and that some have been on sale at Rouen, of which the Archduke Albert, Count of Flanders, gave information to our Lord King Philip III.

* De l'Isle, in his map "L'Amérique Septentrionale" (Paris, 1700), places north of the Missouri at 40° N. "Quivira habité par les Aixaos," probably traceable to Benavides and Peñalosa. In Spanish pronunciation Aixaos and Ahijaos are the same. Three years later De l'Isle, in his "Carte du Canada" (Paris, 1703), gives in the same place La Hontan's fictitious Long River with the Essanapes as one of the tribes. Benavides, p. 91, distinguishes between the kingdom of Quivira and that of the Aixaos, and makes them 30 or 40 leagues east of the Xumanas. By 1743 ideas as to Quivira had become very vague. Bellin, in his Carte de l'Amérique Septentrionale (Shea's Charlevoix, i. p. 100), has between the head-waters of the Missouri and the Pacific, far to the northwest of Santa Fe: "Ici doivent etre les pays de Quivira et de Taguaio dont on n'a aucune connaissance certaine."

For which reason his Majesty, wishing to rid himself of that English settlement, ordered all the harbors of Virginia to be sounded, confiding this conquest to Garibay; and it was in this part, about the northward, that the great English pirate, Ser Thomas, drew the great wealth of gold, who with incredible boldness and pride entered London by the Thames with his rigging and sails of silk, and who landed and placed in the square at London so much treasure that Queen Elizabeth herself went to see it with her court; and this store of gold was obtained by this pirate in one of those rivers which descend from the northward near this land, which has all its population running from north to south; and this avarice has induced the English to try and penetrate inland, and from their not knowing how to make war on Indians they have always come off worst, and this has so alarmed them that they dare not join battle with them.

We have had here some Indians, natives of those parts, and who have been in that kingdom of the Ahijados (which is Thegüayo), who gave clear indications of them and of their wealth, and of the

Dutch who are settled there near Virginia, and that they had also been in the provinces of the Otocomanes and Aitacomanes, where the abundance of silver and gold is such that all the vessels for their use are of silver, and in some cases of gold ; and the same was stated, according to trustworthy persons, by that Indian Michael, a native of this kingdom of Theguayo, who accompanied Don Juan de Oñate, Adelantado of New Mexico, who was carried to Spain by the Maese de Campo Vicente de Saldivar, and in Madrid he presented to our Lord the King this same information. His Majesty rewarded the services of the Maese de Campo with the habit of Santiago ; and although these certain and great riches are heard like dreams amid the Spanish indifference, among foreign nations they are very earnest and tested by evidence and great interest. With this view they overlook no spot on those coasts of the South and North Sea that they do not explore and see, knowing and valuing better than the Spaniard the many large, rich pearls of this our neighboring Gulf of California and in the bays of our rivers, and especially in those of Quivira, whence the Indians gave so many (though inferior ones) to the Señor Adelantado, and here they ordinarily bring them to us to buy, and we have seen many as large as peas, and much rich amber which they do not esteem, and they bring it in fragrant masses for their gratification.

The two Casiques proceeded to say that further on, towards the North and under, beyond the towns of their nation, there were other rich and powerful peoples with great towns, which would require three days to pass them; and all these provinces and the lands which we have seen are fertile, abundant, fresh, and with great fruit trees, especially nut trees of three different kinds, and very full of cibolas, and with a great lake surrounded by great cities and villages of splendid, rich, and warlike people.

The account of these casiques and the questions of Don Diego and the Father chaplains lasted till midnight, at which hour they were sent to sleep; but they, seeing themselves alone and among such strange and foreign folk, and that their enemies, the Escanxaques, were so near, fled and crossed the river to their city, which at sunrise was depopulated and without inhabitants, because their enemies, the Escanxaques, without being observed by our men, slipped off and attacked the city, killing, burning, and destroying all they could; on which surprise his Lordship ordered the army to cross the river, and it was forded with difficulty, as it was still night, and he encamped at the entrance of the town, which is situated on the delightful banks of another river, which runs through the midst of it, and the houses and streets are on both banks, and the shape of the buildings for the most part is round, two, three, and four stories, covered with straw with wonderful skill, and the framework of Coleo, Curcúra, or Otaté, which are all three names of a solid cane, strong and full of knots, of which walking-sticks are usually made, which does not grow in warm climates; and, as we observed in what we saw, they plant twice a year, as some fields were ready to harvest and others were planting. We could find no Indian to act as interpreter, as all had fled, fearing the great fury of their enemies, the Escanxaques, whom they supposed to be favored by and in alliance with our men, and to arrest the conflagration of the city it was necessary for the army to march in two bodies, and that the one with the Maese de Campo should spend most of the day in keeping back the Escanxaques.

The next morning the army marched through the town some two leagues, and, having counted some thousands of houses, halted on the bank of another river, which also entered it; and it was remarked that every quarter of a league, a little more or less, highways entered the city of sixteen paths and some of more, well beaten and even, which came down from the lofty range, which was some six leagues distant from the buildings.

From this point the Señor Adelantado sent a squad of twenty-five soldiers with the Sergeant Major Francis de Madrid to go and explore all the town, without their being able to reach the end of the streets, and when furthest on they discerned more of the town, and more smokes on the ridge, which ran along the right side of the city towards the north.

Before arriving at this town we passed many very large rivers, which abound in various kinds of fish, such as bochinetes, cackerel, matalotes, silurus, sardines, moxarras, trout, eels, pipefish, whitefish, tope, mussels, shrimp, and others, and most of these rivers very deep to run asequias for irrigation, and the soil black, strong, fertile, and covered with grass, and in conclusion all the plain from the city of Quivira to the ridge, which must be six or seven leagues, seemed a paradise; and Señor Don Diego, seeing that it was useless to follow men who fled, and not knowing whether the vehicle would find passage, and especially as he had no orders to make any new discoveries, from that part turned back to these provinces on the 11th of June (Day of St. Barnabas the Apostle), and as he came marching along the Escanxaques Indians came out to meet him arms in hand, and, ungrateful for the kindness which had been shown them, joined with others of their nation, who formed a body of more than seven thousand and had returned to enter the city at the front; and although they were summoned peaceably, they would not hearken, and it became necessary to fight; and in a bloody battle fought against them the Señor Adelantado killed more than three thousand of them in less than three hours, and the rest took flight, having experienced the superiority of balls over arrows, although these they discharged in torrents, so that they seemed to be storms of hail.

There were on this expedition men of various nations in Europe, Asia, Africa, and America, and all unanimously declared that they had never seen so fertile, pleasant, and agreeable a country as that, and they are awaiting his Lordship's return with new orders from his Majesty and the reward of the title of Duke thereof, Marquis of Farara, and that of Count of Santa Feé de Peñalosa, which he has so well merited.

Four months thereafter there came to this kingdom a leading Casique of Quivira with more than seven hundred Indians and trains of dogs loaded with chamois and buckskins and other skins, and went to see the Señor Adelantado, and gave his Lordship thanks for the punishment he had inflicted on their enemies the Escanxaques, and gave again accounts of the great rich cities inland and notable things about them and with his finger he drew on the ground a map as well of his own land and the towns near them as of the lands of his enemies, and others with their rivers, mountains and plains, cities and towns of different styles of building, and their plains full of cibolas and other different kinds of animals unknown in our Europe, with other things of strange greatness.

All this, as the Cacique depicted it on the ground, Don Diego ordered to be copied on paper to transmit to his Majesty, and the Cacique begged his Lordship to return to his country, where he should be better received than the first time, and as guides he gave two Indians of his company, who were to conduct him by a shorter and better route. He set out pleased and content with the honor his Lordship paid him, giving him a suit with gold lace and a hat with plumes, which he admired, as those they use are no finer, and a gilt shortsword which this savage chief esteemed notably.

By the aforesaid it is clearly seen that all the information given to the blessed Father Francis de Escobar, and to the Adelantado of New Mexico, Don Juan de Oñate, when he conquered this kingdom, and that given in this expedition to the East and Quivira, all tend to the same part, which is under the North, and that given us by the Thaos Indians and those of the Apaches nation their neighbors, who are more to the Northeast, are all the same; and that this rich and populous northeast land begins in the spacious plains of Quivira, 150 leagues from here, and continues almost as far till the point where the settled part begins; and from this the greatness of the country and towns towards under the North is incredible, all surrounded by the sea on all sides, and according to the report of those dwelling on the south sea, the sea turns at the point of that range of California, encircling the land towards the Northwest, North, and Northeast, and they say that they know that it reaches there, and that they presume it passes on, because they do not find any ultimate term, and they give an account of the very rich lake of Copala and its Mexicans, who on all its great circuit have many towns, and from this lake to the northwest they place all the nations mentioned in the expedition of the South Sea, and those of Quivira who live to the East say that the sea is ten leagues distant behind the great Sierra, that it is eight from the city of Taracari, and that thence it runs to the northeast, north, and northwest, which is the same gulf of California, so that from Quivira we know by evident proof that the Sea encircles and embraces all that land in those four directions: from the east to the northeast, north, and northwest.

And this very lofty Sierra keeps always following it, and the inhabitants of those regions do not know where it terminates, and if from this port of New Mexico we strike to the east, north, or west, in every direction we shall reach the sea in less than 250 leagues, in consequence of the uniform circle which that of California makes in the said four directions, and the whole strength of the riches and great towns of this Sierra near the Great Quivira, and more to the East, are in the direction of the sea, the slopes towards which are settled with many cities of curious buildings, three stories high, and so the whole land runs almost hugging the coast, very rich and well inhabited, till the great lake of Copala, from whose mines come the rich gold stones which the Governor bought by barter; and although all this peopled country is as stated in length, it cannot have more than fifty leagues' breadth, like the kingdom of Portugal, which though so extensive that it runs from the confines of the kingdom of Galicia to Algarbe, is yet only thirty leagues wide. And for this expedition and discovery to be shorter, we must go, according to what the Quiviras say, by the Thaos, which is the shortest and most direct route, and the towns are nearer, and can be understood, and it is also held for certain that the nine great towns which are seventy leagues hence in a straight line from the Tahos, to the north, are the beginning of those extensive kingdoms, and that thence the settled country continues and the further you advance the more numerous are the hamlets.

The preceding is proved also by the greatness and richness of that northeast land in the interior by the statements which we have also read in the expedition made by the Maestre de Campo Vincent de Saldivar, which he made to the south sea by order of his uncle the Adelantado Don Juan de Oñate, with a pilot and all the requisites to build a bark or boat, ordering him when he reached the River of Good Hope (or del Tison,* which is the same) he should not descend the river which runs north south to the Gulf of California, which is where they went the first time, but that passing the river and the great mountain range, along whose skirts it bears its current to the south sea, they should from that sierra descend to the sea and seek the island of the Gigantic women, so called, and discover the Laguna of Copala, where the richest mines of Moctegsuma † are, which, with help of God, we hope to see discovered by the Lord Adelantado, as has been written.

* The Gila.
† Sagean makes the King of the Acaaniba descend from Montezuma, p. 12.

ACCOUNT

Of a Previous Expedition by the Maestre de Campo Vincent de Saldivar.

In the year 1618 the Maestre de Campo, Vincent de Saldivar, set out on this expedition of discovery with 47 soldiers well equipped, and with them Father Friar Lazarus Ximenez, of the order of our Seraphic Father Saint Francis, and passing through these same populous and civilized tribes till the last of Moq, and marching through those uninhabited parts fifteen days more, they arrived at the Rio de Buena Esperanza or del Tison, at which place they found themselves to be at 36½°; and, marching two days up the same northward, with a very good guide who offered to conduct them, they arrived at a small town, and, inquiring as to the land in the interior, they told them such great things of it, as those west on the coast of the South sea and California had told them, and as those on the east in Quivira told us, which encouraged all to pursue their march, but as among other things they told them that as they advanced they would meet some terrible nations of giants, so huge and extraordinary that one of our men on horseback was small compared to them, and that they fired very large arrows, it did not seem to Saldivar that he led a force sufficient to cope with such a multitude of barbarous tribes, so that he determined to return, fearing some disaster such as befell Captain Humaña and others; and although this resolution was opposed by Father Lazarus and most of the soldiers, it did not avail, although twenty-five of them volunteered, asking leave to enter and explore the land, the Maestre de Campo would not grant it to them, fearing that all would lose their lives: on the contrary he ordered the expedition to halt and return; and executing this prudent determination, and while they were packing the baggage, the earth at that point showed great feeling by a terrible and awful earthquake, which seemed to play with the most solid mountains, so did it move them, prostrating on the ground the loaded beasts and the men, leaving nothing in its place, heaven showing mysteriously by this earthquake the coward heart of those who turned back from the very gates of that fertile, rich, and spacious land, for, in the general opinion, all that has been hitherto conquered and settled under the name of America is sombre compared to what is contained in this new part of the New World, threatened with conquest by the French who border on it, and by the English and Dutch who so greatly desire it, although neither one nor the other will obtain it, because they are ignorant of the art of conquering, that being reserved to the valor and address of our nation and the Portuguese, although at that time our men dared not proceed to view it, even to undeceive themselves.

Then Father Friar Lazarus exclaimed, they say, crying in a loud voice with wonderful grief: O Spaniards! how indignant is the earth at our lack of valor, and we are not; but I believe and hold for certain that our good God and Lord reserved the conquest of the mainland for the illustrious Pedrarias de Avila, son of the Count of Puñon-Rostro, and that of Peru for the most fortunate Francis Pizarro, and that of Chile for the illustrious Peter Gutierrez de Valdivia, and that of the navigation of the South Sea for the famous Don Diego de Ocampo; and that of Mexico for the renowned Fernan Cortés; reserves this for the excellent Don Diego Dionisio de Peñalosa, who as great-grandson of the three greatest knights (Pedro Arias Davila, Pedro de Valdivia, Diego de Ocampo) and best soldiers of the five mentioned, and who married the granddaughter of the ever-victorious Marquis del Valle, Duke of Terranova (Fernan Cortés), seems to reproduce the valor of such excellent heroes, since in his time we see overcome so many difficulties, and the way discovered to propagate the gospel, extend the monarchy, and increase the commerce of Christendom, making his house more illustrious by his sword with the titles of Marquis and Count of fair cities which he has founded from the cornerstones, and who aspires to that of Duke to become as illustrious of himself as the most excellent of his glorious progenitors, to whose titles of Marquis, Count, and Viscount he is the lawful heir, as of their zeal in honoring and patronizing our Seraphic order, as so Christian a knight and our Brother by Letters Patent from our most Reverend Father Commissary-General Friar Diego Zapata.

NOTE.

This document is copied literally from that which Father Guardian, Preacher and Commissary, Friar Nicholas de Freytas, wrote with his own hand, the original of which was forwarded to his Majesty with the printed "Memorial" of the Señor Adelantado * in the year 1663, the result of which is awaited, to achieve so glorious an enterprise giving treasures to the crown of Spain to dominate the globe, for the glory of God, in whose mighty hand are all things past, present, and to come, and of his Blessed Mother, the Virgin Mary, Our Lady conceived without stain of original sin.

Known nations who trade with the Quiviras and Ahijaos of the kingdom of Theguayo, near the lands of the French

* Señor Icazbalceta, of Mexico, whose bibliographical knowledge is well known, in a kind reply to a question as to this "Memorial," says : " Before receiving your letter I had no intimation of the existence of the said 'Memorial,' inasmuch as I have never seen it or found it cited by any author. I have friends who might give me some light, and no one knows the book. These memorials, although printed, are extremely rare, because they were not generally printed for the public, but only to distribute among high personages ; the edition was consequently very small."

which they call Canada on the banks of the river Saint Laurence, which our Indians declare to be very large and navigable to the sea, are the following: Escanxaques, who make a great quantity of white and well-dressed buckskins and very many chamois and other skins, and are situated at 40° latitude. They have on the north the Land of Fire,* and higher up the Fresh Water Lake,† which is, they say, of excessive size, and in it empties another lake which they call Puela,‡ in which there is a mineral island of rich copper, base gold, or excellent brass.

Marching from the Escanxaques towards New France, there are the Neuters, Antovorinos, Raised Hair,§ of the Tuft,‖ of Perun ' (an herb which they sell among them and use like tobacco), and the fiercest the Hiroquees,** of whom they say proverbially: To ten Hiroquees four of the Tuft, and to these two Escanxaques, and to ten Escanxaques one Apache; all of whom are populous, and some of their towns surrounded by palisades after the fashion of the Sunis of our Cibola.

Note that according to El Hacho,†† an Estanxaque petty king, there is no great distance from the Hiroquees to the kingdom of New France, which by another name is called Acanadá, so that it would not be difficult to sack the chief towns.

Note, too, that after passing the lofty sierra of the Escanxaques eight or ten days' march there are settlements of white and red people, who are doubtless English of Virginia or New England.

---

* Country of the Mascoutins.   † Lake Huron.   ‡ Green Bay.   § Chippewas.
‖ Hurons.   ¶ Tionontates, or Petun tribe.   ** Iroquois.
†† Sagean, p. 18, gives Hagaaren as King of his Acaaniba.

84 THE DISCOVERY

May our Lord in his infinite mercy grant that our Governor and Captain General may by his valor and skill remove all the difficulties raised by those who are not accustomed to overcome the impossible, as his Lordship is, for whom Divine Providence has reserved it in its secret bosom till this time. *Quia omnia in tempore suo quærentur.*

NOTE ADDED BY THE COUNT OF PEÑALOSA.

Your Paternity has not mentioned in this transcript the etymology of the names of the land inhabited by the French, by which the opinion contrary to that of the Governor of Biscay is proved, because they call all this land of New France, Canada, a term corrupted in their manner of speaking, because they should say Aca-nada, the contempt shown by the Spaniards, who abandoned it as poor; and the vanity of what the French author parades, whom the said Governor cites to me as being the first who selected the site where the capital of Aca-nada was founded. It is also an unsupported presumption, because the Indian savages call it by the very same name that he says, it is known to have been a site selected by Spaniards, whose language the French captain was ignorant of, as we are of his: it is, then, Estadaca, which was doubtless the persuasion (to settle there) of the commander of the Expedition; and the Frenchman having found the ruins, settled there, and they call it Quebec. I do not know what it means, although you may look in the Vocabulary of these two languages which I sent to your Paternity and Father Guevara, who is a Catalan, perhaps knows it.

AUTO DE LA FE

En Santo Domingo, Año de 1668, *Febrero.**

Viernes 3 se celebró auto particular de la fe en el Convento de Santo Domingo, en que salieron penetenciados once reos, y entre ellos un Fernando de Tolosa, cuyo principio fué herrador y despues fue cirujano, por haberse fingido ministro del Santo Tribunal, y en la iglesia del pueblo de Ixmiquilpan puesto dosel y haber hecho suspender el santo Sacrificio de la Misa para que se leyese en su presencia un edicto supuesto por él, en el cual decia haberle dado autoridad´ el Santo Tribunal para absolver de amancebamiento, dandole un tanto por cada año, y al recibirlo decia: ni recibas cohecho ni pierdas derecho. Dieronle doscientos azotes en esta ciudad, y otros doscientos en el pueblo de Ixmiquilpan, y desterrado á las Islas Filipinas. Asi mismo salió en dicho Auto D. Diego de Peñaloza, gobernador del Neuvo Mexico, por suelto de lengua contra sacerdotes y señores inquisidores, y algunos disparates que tocaban en blasfemias. Salió en cuerpo (que lo tenia mui bueno), vestido de terciopelo negro; el pelo (que era propio y crecido) muy peinado; las medias arrugadas; puños que se usaban de puntas de Flandes muy grandes, que parece se compusó á propósito, sin capa ni sombrero, con vela verde en la mano; causó mucha lástima.— *Diario de Sucesos notables, escrito por el Licenciado D. Antonio de Robles, y comprende los años de* 1665 *á* 1703. En los " Documentos para la Historia de México " (México, 1853, 8°, I. ii. pp. 56–7).

* Señor Icazbalceta adds to his other favors a copy of this sketch of Peñalosa's appearance in the Auto de la Fe.

AUTO DE LA FÉ

At Santo Domingo, February, 1668.

On Friday, 3d, a special auto de la fe was celebrated at the convent of Santo Domingo, in which eleven convicts came forth as penitents, and among them one Ferdinand de Tolosa, who was originally a farrier and afterwards became a surgeon, for having pretended to be a Minister of the Holy Tribunal, and set up a canopy in the church of the town of Ixmiquilpan, and for having caused the holy sacrifice of the Mass to be suspended in order that an edict forged by him might be read in his presence, which recited that the Holy Tribunal had given him authority to absolve for concubinage, on giving him so much for each year; and on receiving it he said: Receive no bribe, and lose no right. They gave him two hundred lashes in this city, and two hundred more in the town of Ixmiquilpan, and he was banished to the Philippine Islands. There also came forth in the said Auto D. Diego de Peñaloza, governor of New Mexico, for unrestrained language against priests and lords inquisitors, and some absurdities that bordered on blasphemy. He came out in a shirt, which was very fine; dress of black velvet; his hair (which was his own and long) well dressed; his stockings wrinkled; very large hand-ruffles of Flemish point-lace, then used, so that apparently he attired himself on purpose, without cloak or hat, with a green candle in his hand. He excited much compassion.—*Diary of Antonio de Robles*, Documentos para la Historia de México, I. ii. pp. 56–7.

QUIVIRA

And the Expeditions to It.

The point reached by Peñalosa's expedition is not at once apparent from the vague way in which the chronicler, Father Freytas, writes. At first he makes the march east, but later on he speaks of the country as northeast of Santa Fe, and this is apparently more correct, as he states that, according to the Indians, the route by way of Taos would have been more direct. If this theory is adopted Quivira lay east of the Missouri River while coming from the north, and before it turns its course to the eastward. The distance from Santa Fe would not be far from the truth, and the trail followed would be one much travelled subsequently.

The short distance advanced along the river after the bend, and the fact that the town was on a river entering the Missouri from the east, seem to point to the rich lands on the Platte. The high ridge would be the line of bluffs enclosing the bottom-lands along the Missouri.

All the early accounts make Quivira beyond a great river which Minet and de l'Isle, as we have seen, regarded as the Missouri. This idea is supported by the opinion of Father Escalante, a very intelligent missionary explorer of the last century, who, writing to Father Morfi, the historian of Texas, expresses the belief that Quivira was the country of the Pananas (Pawnee) Indians, they being the first pueblos northeast of Santa Fe. Tehuayo he believed to be the original seat of the Tihuas, Tehuas, and other tribes of New Mexico. When the Spaniards first occupied New Mexico they found Apaches on all the frontiers of that territory, those on the bison plains being called Apaches Vaqueros. In the last century the Comanches had completely dislodged the Apaches from the buffalo country, and the Utes had forced them from the north and northwest frontiers of New Mexico, two Shoshone nations displacing an Athapascan one. This leads to the belief that the nation found with the Apaches by Oñate were the Comanches, and that they are the Escanxaques of Peñalosa, they having by that time replaced the Apaches on the plains.

Whether the Quivira tribes were the same at different times is of course uncertain. The houses found by Oñate and Peñalosa differ from each other and from those of the Pawnees; and unfortunately no words in the language of Quivira have been preserved.

There were two Quiviras,* each being distinctly described by Father Benavides, the western one on p. 106, and the eastern one, that near the Aixaos, on p. 91. The latter is the one to which Peñalosa penetrated, as Coronado had done a century before. There were several successive expeditions to the

* The name Quivira, or, as first written, Quebira, does not seem to come from any Indian dialect, and, as it was applied to supposed great kingdoms in different directions, may be in its origin simply the Arabic word Quebir, *great*. Estevanico, the survivor of Narvaez's party, who served as a guide to Father Mark of Nice, may have used it to express the points where he heard of powerful cities. The word would be familiar to Spaniards. Guadalquivir is the Arabic Wad'-al-quebir (River the Great); a city in Morocco was known to the Spaniards as Alcazar-el-Quibir (Palace the Great). Luis del Marmol Carvajal, lib. iii. ch. 41. So, too, the port of Oran, captured by Cardinal Ximenes in 1509, was called by the Spaniards Mazalquivir (Mers-el-Kebir).

OF QUIVIRA. 91

Quivira in the Northeast. The first was that of Coronado in 1542. One account fixes the river at 36° N. and Quivira itself at 40°. Coronado was accompanied by the Franciscan John de Padilla, who, after the return of the expedition to the Rio Grande, set out with a lay brother and a small party to found a mission at Quivira, but the missionaries and most of their people were killed by the Indians.* Tartadax was then king or chief at Quivira.

Davis, in his "Conquest of New Mexico" (p. 273), refers to an expedition of Oñate to this Quivira in 1599, but he drew his information from some compilation which had evidently used and misplaced the document of Freytas. There is a report to the King of Spain, written evidently about 1601, in which Oñate's Quivira expedition is thoroughly discussed with a view of enabling his Majesty to decide whether it would be advisable to incur expense for further exploration. This document gives a summary of Oñate's account, but complains of its obscurity and want of definite distances or landmarks. There is no allusion to the Escanxaques or any of the matter given by Davis.

According to this document Oñate marched through the Apaches, and over prairies, and by streams and rivers for two hundred leagues till they met a hunting camp of Indians like the Apaches. A little further on they came to a larger Indian population in a fixed town of considerable size, with houses of straw laid on thick rods. This town ran along for several leagues. Here his men compelled Oñate to turn

---

* See account of his expedition in Ramusio, 1565 (iii. p. 359); Cieza de Leon, Venice, 1565 (ii. p. 303); B. Smith, "Coleccion de Documentos," p. 147; Barcia, "Ensayo Cronologico," p. 21; Torquemada, "Monarquia Indiana," iii. p. 610; Castañeda de Najera, pt. ii. c. 8; pt. iii. c. 4.

back. A committee who examined Oñate's vague account concluded that he must have gone north of 40°.

Two Franciscans, Father Peter Ortega, Guardian of Santa Fe, and Father Alonso Yanés, advanced one hundred leagues into the Apache country, and then went fifty leagues east and fifty north, reaching finally a very large river, which they called San Francisco; but their Apache guides were afraid to proceed any further and the religious returned.

Another expedition eastward from Santa Fe was that of the Missionary Fathers Juan de Salas and Diego Lopez to the Xumana nation. Benavides, who narrates the miraculous conversion of this tribe, says: "Setting out from the city of Santa Fe, the centre of New Mexico, which is at 37°, passing through the Apache nation of the Vaqueros (Bison-hunters), you come to the Xumana nation, whose conversion was so miraculous that it is just to relate how it was" ("Memorial," p. 83). De l'Isle, on his map of *L'Amérique Septentrionale* (Paris, 1700), puts the Xumanas and the Japies, a neighboring tribe mentioned by Benavides, north of the Missouri, the Xabotaos being between them and Quivira. See also a tract of 16 pp. commencing, "Tanto, que se sacò de una carta que el R. P. Fr. Alonso de Benavides . . . envió desde Madrid el año de 1631," and the Life of Maria de Agreda prefixed to her "Mistica Ciudad de Dios."

In the year 1606 more than 800 Quivira Indians came to Santa Fe to ask Oñate to aid them against the Ayjaos, who were waging fierce war against them. An Ayjao prisoner was given to the Spaniards, and received the name of Michael. He is frequently referred to in subsequent accounts. The

Quiviras gave great accounts of the wealth of the Ayjaos and of the gold to be found in their country.*

In 1611 Oñate led an expedition southeast and reached a Rio Colorado, which subsequent writers took to be the Palizada, or Mississippi, and near the country of the Caddodachos. This was apparently the Red River.†

All these allusions show that there were several exploring expeditions sent to the north and east of New Mexico, and that intercourse was kept up with tribes of a more sedentary character than the bison-hunting bands.

Col. Meline, author of "Two Thousand Miles on Horseback," assured me that he saw in the archives at Santa Fe several maps showing explorations made from New Mexico in early times. These have all disappeared, as the present Secretary of the Territory, Hon. W. G. Ritsch, informs me. It is to be hoped they fell into the hands of persons who will appreciate their value, though if the statement be true that Gov. Arny sold quantities of the archives for waste paper, they may have perished utterly.

Spaniard and Frenchman were alike groping their way to the Mississippi; but Coronado led the way to the Missouri, and Oñate seems to have approached that river and the lower Mississippi before Nicolet reached the Wisconsin; just as at a later date Peñalosa struck the Missouri before Joliet passed its mouth in his canoe.

The Spaniards kept up expeditions to the Missouri, and in 1719 an expedition from New Mexico under Villazur, guided by a Frenchman, reached the Missouri opposite the towns of

---

* "Relacion imbiada del Nuevo Mexico." Testimony taken by Dn Francis Manuel Nieto de Silba, Governor of New Mexico, dated Oct. 8, 1629.

† Pinos, "Noticias del Nuevo Mexico," p. 5.

curate description of the provinces which he had seen, their abundance, wealth, multitude of Indians who inhabited them, very docile to carry out his intention. The Maese de Campo Don Juan Dominguez de Mendoça, a very experienced captain in those parts, also wrote that he had been in Quivira in the year 1684, and passed as much as sixty leagues from the villages of the Indians, and arrived within twenty leagues of the Tejas, and among other things he averred that it was easy to penetrate and settle the lands; and he offered if they gave him 200 soldiers, with rations and clothes, as far as the river Nueces, which is 400 leagues from Mexico, to bind himself to conquer a great empire, of which he gave some general ideas; and to maintain from the river Nueces onward, with the fruits of the earth, not only 200 men, but 200,000, if it were necessary, for as he had been in those first provinces, without doing any harm to the Indians, he maintained at the cost of the territory all the force he led; and he added that if some of the provinces described by Father Nicholas were settled, New Biscay would remain very free from the insults of the Indians, for, without their perceiving it, they would soon be assailed in the rear from the east, and hemmed in between the old and new settlements, so that they would be speedily reduced. They sent maps as clearly drawn as they could of the new lands and provinces around New Mexico, on the North, East, and West, which only served to eternalize his zeal for the service of God and of the king and to condemn our neglect." *

According to a statement in the manuscript now first published, Peñalosa presented a printed Memorial of his expedi-

* "Ensayo Cronologico," p. 266.

tion to the King of Spain. It was a matter of importance to trace a copy of the work, if possible. No copy is known to exist in any of the great public libraries or in the choice treasures of private collectors in this country, and if Peñalosa left any at Paris, not one has found its way to any of the great libraries in that city, as I learn by inquiries through Mr. E. Dufossé. As the reader has seen, Señor Icazbalceta, one of the best informed historical and bibliographical scholars in Mexico, states that the work is entirely unknown among students in that republic.

There was a possibility that a copy might be found among the rare works possessed by the Real Academia de la Historia of Madrid, or in the library of his Catholic Majesty. Through the kindness of Hon. Frederick T. Frelinghuysen, Secretary of State, and our Minister at Madrid, Hon. Hannibal Hamlin, an application was made to that learned body. The Secretary, Don Pedro de Madrazo, obligingly examined the collections, but has been unable to find a copy of the Memorial.

INDEX.

ACAANIBAS, 59, 77, 83.
Acanada, 83–4.
Agreda, Maria de, 92.
Ahijaos Indians, 34, 65, 51, 82, 90.
Ahijados, 35, 65–6 ; 82.
Aitacomanes, 35, 67.
Aixaos, 65, 90.
Alaman, Disertaciones, 11.
Albert, Count of Flanders, 34, 65.
Albuquerque, 10.
Alburquerque, Francis Fernandez de la Cueva, Duke of, Viceroy of Mexico, 10.
Alcazar-el-Quibir, 90.
Algarbe, 44, 76.
Antovorinos, 52, 83.
Apache Vaqueros, 90, 92.
Apaches, 10, 42, 74, 84, 90–2.
Arequipa, 9.
Arias de Anaya, 8.
Aricaxa, 9.
Arny, Gov., 93.
Athapascan, 90.
Auto de la fé, 87, 88.
Ayjao, 92–3.

BAÑOS, Count de, Viceroy of Mexico, 10.
Barcia, 7, 15, 46, 91, 94.
Barlow, S. L. M., 21.
Barroto, 15.
Bastida, Pedro de la, 94.
Beaujeu, Captain, 8, 21–2.
Bellin, map, 65.

Bénard de la Harpe, 94.
Benavides, Father Alonso de, 57, 65, 90, 92.
Biscay, 53, 84.
Bobadilla, 8.
Briseño, 8.
Briseño y Cordova, Don Alonso, Bishop of Nicaragua, 9.
Buena Esperanza, River of, 45, 77; 47, 78.

CABARET DE VILLERMONT, 8.
Cabrera, 8.
Cachoupins, 15, 19.
Caddodachos, 88.
California, 36, 67 ; 42–3, 45, 74–5, 48, 77.
Callao, 9.
Canada, 34, 51, 65, 83–4 ; origin of name, 54.
Canary Islands, 11.
Cañete, Marquis de, 9.
Castañeda de Nagera, 91.
Cavelier, Abbé John, 22.
Cavellos Realzados (Cheveux relévés), 52, 83.
Cénis, 23.
Charles II., 12.
Charlevoix, 65, 94.
Chicago River, 12.
Chilcota, 10.
Chile, 81.
Chippewas, 83.
Chuncho Indians, 9.

INDEX.

Cibola, 83.
Cieza de Leon, 91.
Clermont College, Paris, 11.
Comanches, 90.
Copala, 43–5, 74, 76–7.
Cordova, 8.
Coronado, 60, 90–1, 93.
Cortes, Fernan, 50, 81.
Creoles, 15.
Cussy, Sieur de, 20–1.
Cuzco, 9.

DAVIS, W. W. H., 91.
De l'Isle, Maps of, 65, 89, 92.
Dominguez de Mendoza Juan, 90 ; Tomé, 27, 58.
Dufossé, E., 96.
Dumont, 94.
Dunbar, John B., 59.
Duran, Fernando, 27, 58.

EL HACHO, chief, 83.
Elizabeth, Queen, 35, 66.
Endehe, 16.
Escalante, Father, 89, 94.
Escalona, Duke of, 8.
Escanxaques Indians, met by Peñalosa, 21, 29; 30, 60, 62; surprise Quivira, 37–8, 68–70; attack Spaniards, 40–1 ; 52, 71–2, 83, 91 ; may be the Comanches, 90.
Escobar, Father Francis de, 42, 74.
Essanapes, 59, 65.
Estadaca, 85.
Estanxaque, 83.
Estevanico, 90.

FARARA, 25, 55 ; Marquis de, 25, 41, 72.
Flibustiers, Fribustiers, 13, 15, 17, 21.

Florida, 12, 16, 65.
Fort St. Louis, 20.
Frelinghuysen, Hon. F. W., 96.
Fresh Water Lake, 83.
Fresno, Marquis de, 12.
Freytas, Father Nicholas de, account of his manuscript, 7, 53 ; notice of, 56 ; Relation of Peñalosa's expedition (Spanish), 25 ; (English), 53 ; mentioned, 27, 37, 51, 57, 68, 82, 85, 89, 91.

GALICIA, 44, 76.
Galveston Bay, 21.
Garibay, 66.
Gigantic women, Isle of, 45, 77.
Gila River, 45, 47, 77–8.
Good Hope River, 77–8.
Grammont, 17.
Green Bay, 52, 83.
Guadalquivir, 90.
Guevara, Father Miguel de, 27, 57 ; 37, 68 ; 54, 85.
Guincame, 16.
Gutierrez de Valdivia, Peter, 50, 81.

HAGAAREN, 83.
Hamlin, Hon. Hannibal, 96.
Harrisse, Henri, 21.
Havana, 10, 15.
Hendehé, 14, 16.
Hiroquees (Iroquois), 52, 83.
Humaña, Captain, 48, 79.
Hurons, 83.

ICAZBALCETA, Sr. J. G., 56, 82, 91.
Illinois, 23, 94.
Iroquois, 83.
Ixmiquilpan, 87, 88.

JAPIES, 92.

INDEX.

Joliet, Louis, 93.

LAGUNA, Marquis de, 15.
La Hontan, 59, 65.
Lake Huron, 52, 83.
Land of Fire, 83.
La Paz, 9.
La Salle, Robert Cavelier, Sieur de, 8, 12, 15, 16, 20-1.
Leiva, John de, Marquis de, 10.
Leon, Don Alonso de, 15.
Les pancaké, 21, 60.
Lima, 8.
London, 34, 66.
Long River, 59, 65.
Lopez, Father Diego, 92 ; Father Nicholas, 94-5.
Los Balbazes, Marquis de, 12.
Los Charcos, 9.
Lucero Godoy, Juan, 28, 58.

MADRAZO, Don Pedro de, 96.
Madrid, 94.
Madrid, Francisco de, 39, 70.
Madrid, Real Academia de Historia, 96.
Mark of Nice, Father, 90.
Margry, Pierre, 8, 16.
Mascoutins, 83.
Maya, Marquis de, 8.
Mazalquivir, 90.
Mechoacan, 10.
Mechon (Huron) Indians, 52, 83.
Meline, Col. James F., 93.
Mendizaval, Don Bernard Lopez de, Governor of New Mexico, 10.
Mendoza, Juan Dominguez, de, 95.
Mexico, 9-11, 14-19, 23 ; Gulf of, 16.
Miguel, an Indian of Theguayo, 35, 67, 92.
Milly River, 59.

Minet, Map by, 21, 60, 89.
Mingues, Father John, 94.
Mischipi River, 29, 59.
Mississippi, 15-6, 21, 23, 93-4.
Missouri River, 89, 92-3.
Missouris, 94.
Moctegsuma, 45, 77.
Molina, Count de, 12.
Monclova, Count de, 15.
Montalegre, Marquis de, 10.
Moq, 47, 78.
Morel, Mr., 8, 22.
Morfi, Father, 89.
Morocco, 90.

NAVARRETE, Martin F., 7, 46.
Neuter Indians, 52, 83.
New Biscay, 10, 14-15, 16-21, 95.
New England, 53, 84.
New Mexico, 10, 17, 23, 36, 67, 75, 92.
Nicolet, John, 93.
Nieto de Silba, Francis Manuel, 93.
Noriega, Miguel de, Captain, 27, 58.
Nueces River, 95.
Nueva España, 28, 58.

OCAMPO, 8.
Ocampo, Diego de, 8, 50, 81.
Ochoa y Zarate, Don Andres de, 15.
Omasuyos, 9.
Oñate, Juan de, 35, 67 ; 42, 74, 77; 45, 91-3.
Oran, 90.
Ortega, F. Peter, 92.
Osages, 94.
Otocomanes, 35, 67.

PADILLA, F. John de, 91.
Palizada, 93-4.
Panama, 9.
Pananas (Pawnees) 89, 90, 94.

INDEX.

Panuco, 16-18, 20.
Parkman, Francis, 21.
Paris, 22-3.
Parral, 10-11, 14.
Pawnees, 89.
Payta, 9.
Pedrarias de Avila, 8, 50, 81.
Peñalosa, Diego Dionisio de, Account of, 8; born in Lima, *ib.*; governor of several provinces in Peru, 9; Regidor and Alcalde of La Paz, *ib.*; Alcalde of Cuzco, *ib.*; military services, *ib.*; leaves Peru, wrecked, *ib.*; favorably received in Mexico, 10; employments, *ib.*; Governor of New Mexico, *ib.*; defeats Apaches, founds two cities, *ib.*; sets out on exploring expedition for the east and Quivira, 27, 37; reaches river Mischipi, 29, 39, 69, 90; enters Quivira, 31; defeats Escanxaques, 40; titles aspired to, 40-1; esteemed by the Franciscans; presents a printed Memorial of his Expedition to the King of Spain, 51, 82; confines the commissary-general of the Inquisition in Mexico, 11; is arrested by the Inquisition in Mexico, 11, 17; condemned, *ib.*; appears as a penitent in an Auto de la Fé, 11, 87, 88; stripped of his property, 11; goes to Teneriffe, 11; London, 12; France, *ib.*; Memoir to the Marquis de Seignelay, 12, 94; Memoir on the Affairs of America, 16-20; part to be taken by him in a new project, 21; La Salle sent out to pave the way for his expedition, 22; his death, 23; fruitless efforts to find a copy of his Memorial, 82, 96.
Peñalossa (Peñalosa), Alonso de, 9.
Peñalossa (Peñalosa), Alonzo Fernandez, 9.
Peñalossa (Peñalosa), Diego de, 8-9.
Peñaloza (Peñalosa), 87-8.
Pen loca (Peñaloça), 21.
Pensacola, 15.
Peru, 8, 9, 17, 28, 58.
Perun (Petun) Indians, 52, 83.
Pes, Don Andres de, 15.
Philip III., King of Spain, 34, 65.
Philippine Islands, 87-8
Pieño en Rostro (Puñon Rostro), 8.
Pinelo, 7, 46.
Pinos, 93.
Pizarro, Francis, 50, 81.
Platte River, 89.
Portugal, 44, 76.
Puela, 83.
Puñon-rostro, Count of, 8, 50, 81.

QUEBEC, 54, 85.
Quebira, 60, 90.
Quiros, 46.
Quivira, origin of name, 90; Peñalosa's expedition to, 25, 55; Escanxaques give information about, 30, 60; Peñalosa in sight of, 31, 61; pearls in, 36, 67; attacked by Escanxaques, 37, 42-48, 69, 71-2, 74-5; 79, 86, 90; Taracari, chief city of, 28, 58; Tartadax, King of, 88; position assigned to it on Minet's map, 21; on de l'Isle's maps, 65; probable position, 89-96.
Quiviras, Indians, 29, 60; meet Peñalosa, 31; visit Santa Fé, 41; 51, 82, 92-3.

INDEX. 101

Rio Bravo, 12-3, 15-6, 20.
Rio Colorado, 93.
Rio Grande, 60, 91.
Ritsch, Hon. W. G., 93.
Red River, 93.
Robles, Antonio de, 87-8.
Rouen, 34, 65.

Sagean, Matthew, 59, 78.
Saint Domingo, 13, 15, 17, 20-1.
Sainte Barbe, 14, 16.
Saint Lawrence River, 52, 83.
Salas, F. Juan de, 92.
Saldivar, Vicente de, 36, 67 ; 45, 77 ; his expedition, 47, 78.
Salvatierra, Count of, Viceroy of Peru, 9.
San Diego, 14.
San Francisco River, 92.
San Juan de Guincame, 14, 16.
Santa Barbara, 14, 16.
Santa Fe, 27, 57, 65, 89-90, 92-3.
Santa Fe de Peñalosa, 41, 72.
Santo Domingo, Convent of, 87, 88.
San Yldefonso, Convent of, 27, 57.
Seignelai, Mr. de, 7, 8, 12, 16, 22, 26.
Sessa, Duke de, 8.
Shoshones, 90.
Smith, Buckingham, 7, 46, 91.
Sombrerette, 14, 16.
Soñora, 14.
Spain, 12.
Stoddard, 94.
Sunis, 83.

Tahos, 44, 76.
Taguaio, 65.
Taos, 89.
Taracari, 28, 58, 75.
Tartadax, King of Quivira, 91.
Tehuas, 90.

Tehuayo, 90.
Tejas, Texas, 15, 21-3, 94-5.
Teoas Indians, 57.
Terranova, Duke of, 50, 81.
Thames, 34, 66.
Thaos, 42, 44, 74, 76.
Thegüayo, 35, 65-7 ; 51, 82, 90.
Thevenot, 7.
Thomas, Sir, 34, 66.
Tihuas, 90.
Tionontates, 83.
Tison (Gila) River, 45, 47, 77, 78.
Tonty, Chevalier de, 23.
Tolosa, Ferdinand de, 87, 88.
Torquemada, Father, 86.

Utes, 90.

Valdivia, 8.
Valdivia, Pedro de, 8.
Valle, Marquis del, 50, 81.
Van Horn, 17.
Vera Cruz, 10, 14, 17-8.
Verdugo, 8.
Villazur, 93.
Virginia, 34, 53, 65-7.

Wisconsin River, 93.

Xabotaos, 92.
Ximenes, Cardinal, 90.
Ximenez, Father Lazarus, 47-9 ; 78-80.
Xiquilpa, 10.
Xumanas, 65, 92.

Yanés, Father Alonso, 92.
York, Duke of, 12.
Yriarte, Bernardo de, 7, 46.
Yucatan, 15.

Zacatecas, 10.
Zapata, F. Diego, 51, 82.
Zarate Salmeron, 59.

www.ingramcontent.com/pod-product-compliance
Lightning Source LLC
Chambersburg PA
CBHW021949160426
43195CB00011B/1293